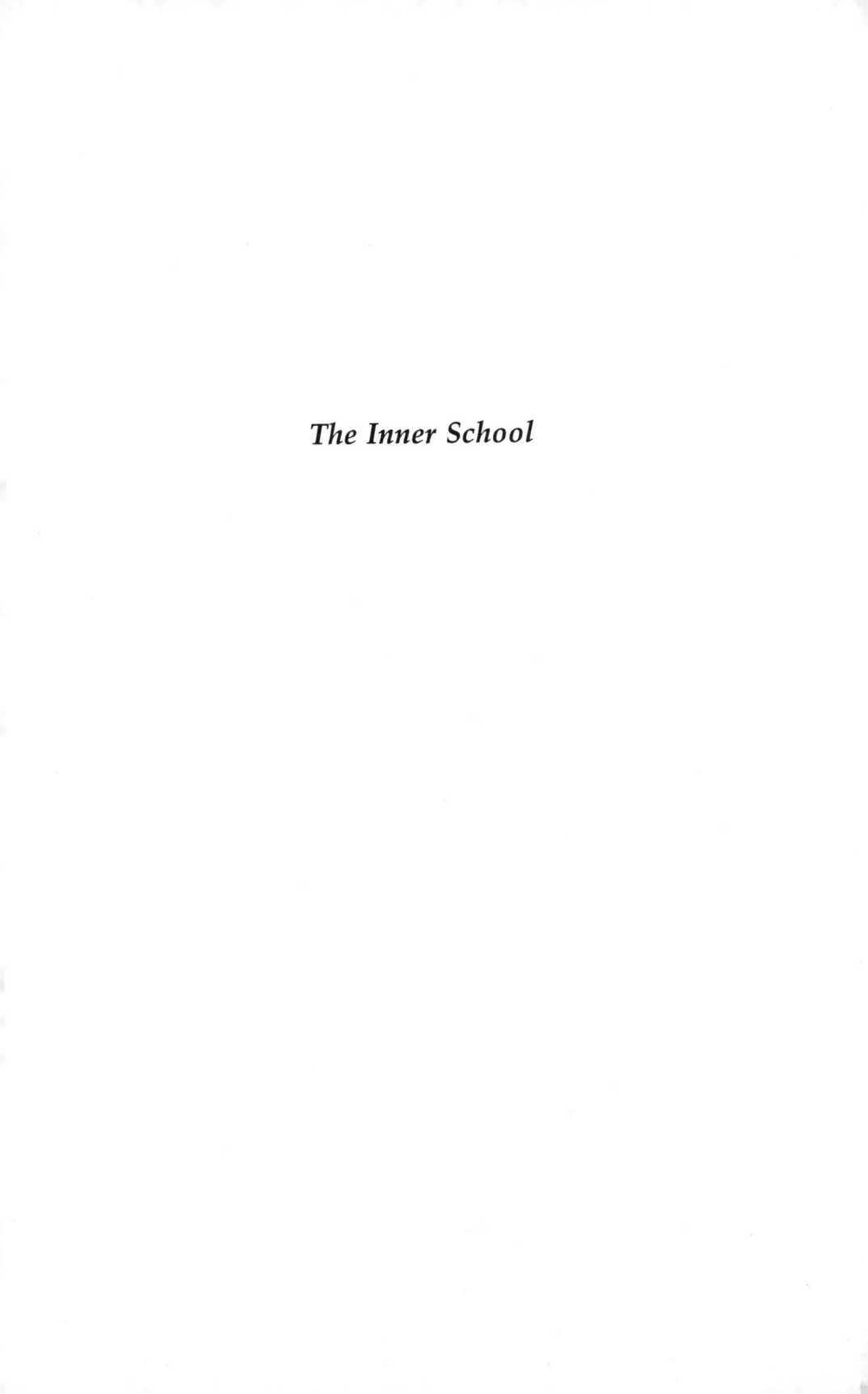

The Inner School

The Inner School
Esoteric Sufi Teachings

Interpretations of the *Gathas, Gathekas, Githas, Sangathas* and *Sangithas* of Hazrat Inayat Khan

Hidayat Inayat Khan

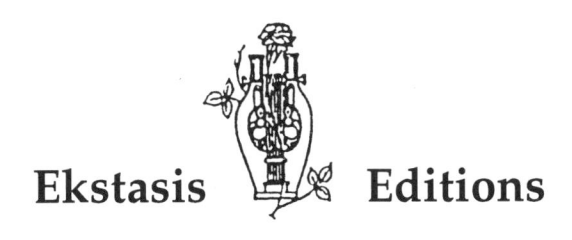

Ekstasis Editions

Canadian Cataloguing in Publication Data

Khan, Hidayat Inayat, 1917-
    The inner school

        ISBN 0-921215-98-3

        1. Sufism. I. Title.
        PS8575.C64M9   1996   2971'.4   C96-910390-5

Copyright © 1996 Hidayat Inayat Khan
All rights reserved.
Editor for the press: Carol Ann Sokoloff

Cover: Dargah of Hazrat Inayat Khan, New Delhi, India

Published in 1996 by
Ekstasis Editions Canada Ltd.   **Ekstasis Editions**
Box 8474, Main Postal Outlet   Box 571
Victoria, B.C. V8W 3S1   Banff, Alberta T0L 0C0

Contents

Introduction / 9

Gathekas / 11

Gathas / 25

Githas / 63

Sangathas / 89

Sangithas / 95

Interpretations / 101

Index of Subjects

The Sufi Message / 13
The Esoteric School / 13
Universal Worship / 14
Brotherhood and Sisterhood / 14
The Spirit of Guidance / 14
Awakening of the Heart / 15
The Aim of the Sufi / 15
The Purpose of Life / 16
Tuning the Ego / 17
The Alchemy of Happiness / 17
The Art of Personality / 18, 51
Superstitions, Customs and Belief / 27
Insight / 33
Symbology / 38
Breath / 45
Morals / 49
Everyday Life / 55
Metaphysics / 59
Attainment / 65
Psychology / 67
Mysticism / 69
Health / 70
Uruj and Nazul / 73
Polarity in Breath / 75
Esotericism / 76
Concentration / 80
Meditation / 83
Spirit Phenomena / 85
The Individual as Seed of God / 103
Reincarnation (Here. Now and Hereafter) / 111
Light and Life / 115
The Mystery of Breath (Shagal) / 116

The Dervish and the King's Procession

A dervish was sitting in meditation, right in the middle of the road along which the Maharaja's procession was due to pass. Crowds of people were running in all directions to have a glimpse of the royal carriage, pushing against the dervish in their rough movements. The dervish sat impassively in their midst, saying only, "That is why."

Soon came the Maharaja's body guards, shouting loudly at the dervish to move out of the way. The dervish showed no other reaction than to repeat the words, "That is why."

Next some courtiers approached the dervish, moving their horses so as to avoid causing him any harm, and the dervish again said, "That is why."

Finally, when the royal carriage reached the spot where the dervish was still sitting, the Maharaja got down and bowed to the dervish, who once again said, "That is why."

When asked what was meant by those words, the dervish replied, "In life, one is really only that which one truthfully is, and one becomes that which one truthfully deserves to be. Destiny is neither planned nor created, it is reached, because one's behaviour is a mirror which faithfully reflects the innermost image of mind, heart and soul."

Introduction

When India's wandering mystic and musician, Inayat Khan, came to Western shores in 1910 to perform the first concerts of Indian music ever heard in America and Europe, he followed the instructions of his own Sufi master to, "harmonize the East and the West through the gift of music." In addition, Sayed Madani had suggested that his remarkable student, honoured as India's finest singer and Veena player, should also endeavour to introduce the spiritual teachings of the East to a Western world ready to awaken to deeper truths. He instructed the young Inayat Khan, who was fully educated in all the traditional Sufi orders of the East as well as in Hindu and Yogic disciplines, to establish in the West a spiritual or Esoteric School, in which those inclined towards mysticism and philosophy might absorb the ancient wisdom of these paths. In keeping with the Sufi idea of speaking in the language and fashion appropriate to a particular situation, Murshid Madani cautioned Inayat Khan against simply creating a Western version of the ancient eastern traditional Sufi orders (such as their own illustrious Chistia order), suggesting instead that this newly created Esoteric School need not even be called Sufi at all, and be available to followers of all religions.

After arriving in America and then settling in first London and then Paris, Pir-o-Murshid Inayat Khan found that his lectures on spiritual subjects began to overtake his musical performances (which had been warmly embraced by such luminaries as composers Debussy and Scriabin), eventually requiring the sacrifice of his greatest pleasure, musical expression, in the service of what the Indian mystic called 'the Sufi Message of Spiritual Liberty.' Pir-o-Murshid Inayat Khan did choose to call the Esoteric School he founded 'Sufi' out of respect for the ancient wisdom tradition which formed the basis of his teachings.

Throughout the relatively brief years in the West (ending with his return to India where he passed away in 1927) the Sufi master, known since his passing as Hazrat Inayat Khan, affected the hearts and souls of thousands of spiritual seekers, establishing his Sufi Movement, the organization designed to accommodate this 'Message of Spiritual Liberty' and its supporters, in America, Holland, France, England, Russia, Italy, Germany, Switzerland, to name only some locations. In the years since his passing, still thousands more have been influenced by the Sufi Message of Hazrat

Inayat Khan, through books and contact with those who have carried on his work in still more countries including Canada, New Zealand, Mexico and Australia, again to name but a few.

In order to create a coordinated system of esoteric training, independent of personalities and able to endure relatively intact through time and translation, Hazrat Inayat Khan, grouped transcriptions of oral teachings for Sufi initiates into a series of unpublished volumes, corresponding to varying degrees of evolution in the subject, to be read aloud in study sessions. The mystic revealed a fondness for the ancient Persian Zoroastrian religion by naming these texts after the scriptures of Zarathustra, calling them the *Gathas*, and the further volumes, *Gathekas, Githas, Sangathas, Sangithas*.

In the past, access to these teachings has been carefully limited to the initiates of the Sufi esoteric schools, although the book known as *The Gathas* did receive publication in the last decade. In this spirit, *Sufi Teachings* author, Hidayat Inayat Khan, son of Hazrat Inayat Khan and current leader of the International Sufi Movement has, in his own highly-condensed fashion, taken the essential teachings of all these volumes and created this book, *The Inner School*, containing summaries of the *Gathekas, Gathas, Githas, Sangathas* and *Sangithas* of Hazrat Inayat Khan. Hidayat writes of these volumes that, "It was Our Master's wish that the originals of these teachings, when they were completed, be placed with others in what he called 'the Children's Bag,' and preserved in the archives of Fazil Manzil (Inayat Khan family home) in Suresnes, France."

'Nirtan' Carol Sokoloff
July 14, 1996
Victoria, British Columbia

Gathekas

The Sufi Message

The Esoteric School

Universal Worship

Brotherhood and Sisterhood

The Spirit Of Guidance

Awakening of the Heart

The Aim of the Sufi

The Purpose of Life

Tuning the Ego

The Alchemy of Happiness

The Art of Personality

Extracts

Seven Aspects
of Brotherhood and Sisterhood

The Sufi Message

Sufism or wisdom, related to the word *Sophia*, is acquired not only through knowledge, but also by the grace of intuition. Sufism is neither a religion nor a cult, neither a doctrine nor a dogmatic institution. Perhaps one could say that Sufism has always been, ever since knowledge was knowledge.

Esoteric schools can be traced at least as far back as the time of Abraham. In Arabia, esoteric schools were known for their metaphysical teachings. In Persia, literature, poetry and music were the source of esoteric inspiration. In India, the esoteric schools were mainly of a meditative character. Although various esoteric schools of East or West may, perhaps, differ slightly in the methods of self-realization, yet all are united in their object, because spirituality does not belong to any one religion nor to just one esoteric school. Wisdom is a divine heritage which is the hidden stream underlying all religious inspiration.

The Esoteric School

The Esoteric School of the Sufi Movement is one of the three main activities through which the Sufi Message of love, harmony and beauty is offered to the world, in recognition of the divine light within the hearts of all God's children. Here, an initiation is given without distinction made as to religion, belief or intellectual background, providing there is an openness to the unity of spiritual ideals.

Very often the word 'initiation' is misunderstood as being a commitment to a secret cult, although originally it designated a resolution taken on the path of self-abnegation. For a Sufi, initiation means taking an initiative and advancing on the path of spiritual liberty, in which each step taken leads to the next, every step being a new initiative, providing a new outlook on life and a broadening of the understanding. In this process, the initiator's guidance is seen as a source of inspiration, with the object of discovering divine truth in the unfolding heart, so that the light within may shine.

Gathekas 13

Universal Worship

The second activity in the Sufi Movement is the Universal Worship, a worship which is destined to be the religion of all religions, where all believers, of every faith, are welcome to worship together in a united worship of all religions. It is a worship offered to the one God of all religions, known and called by different names and attributes, yet the one and greatest ideal which is far beyond limited human understanding.

Brotherhood and Sisterhood

The third activity, called Brotherhood and Sisterhood, is an appeal to the world to unite in tolerance and wisdom, beyond the dogmatic boundaries of caste, creed, race, nation and all types of sectarianism, which are so many lifeless stones constituting rubble rather than the 'Temple of God.'

Brotherhood and sisterhood means speaking to each person in his or her own language; showing understanding for the opinion of others; promoting the unity of religious ideals; offering all that is expected of one, while expecting nothing in return; being a living example of love, harmony and beauty; freeing oneself from the illusion of the self; attuning oneself and one's environment to the divine 'Spirit of Guidance.'

The Spirit of Guidance

The one who says, "My religion is different from yours," does not know what religion means, because there is only one God, one truth, one religion. Call it Hinduism, Buddhism, Christianity or Islam, it does not matter, because all names are like so many drops of one and the same rain pouring down upon humanity without distinction or differences. Therefore, no religion can call itself its own because all religions belong to the same one religion.

For a Sufi, the diversity of names and forms of the world's religious tendencies are like veils covering the phenomena of the 'Spirit of Guidance' manifested at all levels of evolution. This inner guidance is constantly present in the beautiful book of nature's mysteries, which reveals a never-ending 'Message of Love,' providing one's understanding of the relationship between matter and spirit is in harmony with one's feeling heart.

Awakening of the Heart

This explains why one of the great ideals of a Sufi is the awakening of the heart qualities, resulting in a broader outlook. One's view then reaches far beyond concepts of faith and belief, and allows one to offer tolerance to the tragic misunderstandings which divide the earnest followers of various religious and philosophical traditions. When offering as brothers and sisters to partake in carrying the burden of the misunderstandings of others, the Sufi avoids any display of speculative theories, using only the language of the heart to communicate sympathy and dedication in support of the various interpretations of the one ideal of worship.

The solution of the problem of the day is the awakening to the divinity in all beings and, in working for this great cause, one is not only offering service to humanity, but also to God.

The Aim of the Sufi

The aim of the Sufi is to release one's captive soul from the boundaries of the 'I' and 'my' concepts, by merging into the ecstasy of a spiritual ideal. The soul's freedom could be just as peaceful as that ideal, but the Sufi is well aware that as long as there is the limitation of duality, as shown in the concepts of 'I' and 'my,' the soul cannot really be free. This paradox is overcome through the realization that the concepts of 'I' and 'my' are only illusions. What we think of as 'I' is just our own perception of an individual entity functioning as part of an entire network. In the same way, a drop of water is an entity only as long as it is seen as a drop. However, as soon as that drop is poured back into the ocean, it is then all ocean-water. Therefore, for the Sufi, the ideal which releases the soul from its boundaries is, in fact, the soul's own image, the soul itself, which knows not 'I' nor 'my.'

The Purpose of Life

Among the numberless purposes in our lives which, nevertheless, could not be accomplished in a whole lifetime, one might take for granted that the essential ideals which secure a balanced condition between body, mind, heart and soul are those related to the concept of life itself, such as the desire to live fully, the urge for knowledge, the want for power, the longing for happiness and the need for peace.

To the question whether or not a material ideal could lead to an inner purpose, one might say that, seen from the point of view of the 'divine purpose,' even a material ideal could very well be the outcome of a spiritual one. Therefore, every effort towards the fulfilment of one's life's purpose, whether the effort be material or spiritual, whether made consciously or unconsciously, brings one nearer, step by step, to the ultimate goal. Furthermore, this process can be seen as a humble contribution to the fulfillment of the 'divine purpose,' since the entire creation is in a constant state of formation, all according to a central theme.

The purpose of life is not fulfilled only in rising to the greatest heights, but also by diving deep into the deepest depths, whereby the self is lost, but finds itself again as a result of the widening of its sphere of consciousness. It is just like the seed which finds the fulfillment of its purpose when rising as a plant and spreading out in full bloom in the rays of the sun, after having been lowered deep down beneath the ground.

Tuning the Ego

At the level of mystical understanding, according to Sufi esoteric teaching, this could be explained as the process of the tuning of the ego to a higher pitch. One values most that which one has made the greatest efforts to obtain, although, paradoxically, the most valuable achievements are sometimes obtained with the least effort. Unfortunately, one does not always realize the real value of such achievements, unless one has learned the hard way to appreciate all that is bestowed upon one by the grace of God.

There is no experience in life which is worthless. There is not one moment which is really wasted, providing one is wise enough to carefully assemble the bits and pieces of past memories and learn from experience. The self, the conscience, invariably rejoices or suffers unrest from positive or negative thoughts or, when losing hold of itself, becomes radiant, being able then to focus all its creative energy on the reality of the 'Divine Presence.' However, the self is only the channel through which the soul is ultimately the spectator of all happenings, reflected as impressions; and, like a mirror, the reflections perceived do not leave any traces on its pure surface.

The Alchemy of Happiness

Another subject found in Sufi teaching is the 'Alchemy of Happiness' which, as we know from fairy tales, is the use of a magic formula to turn base metal into gold. This mystical legend symbolizes so beautifully the basic principle of the inner school of the Sufis, where deep consideration is offered to the importance of transforming one's gross ego into a humble attitude of respect, awakening one's heart to the consciousness of its privilege in being the 'Temple of God,' radiating God's love onto all who come one's way.

The Art of Personality

This inner consciousness can only be developed along a very thorny path called the 'Art of Personality.' This requires constant efforts to forge the character into a living example of love, harmony and beauty, so that one may be a bringer of happiness. Happiness is the birthright of all beings, although one may not always be conscious of the laws of happiness. These teach one that happiness is only there when one becomes an inspiration of happiness for others. But how might this be accomplished?

It is accomplished through trying to appreciate what is good in another and overlooking that which disturbs one when others are not in accord with one's own thinking; by trying to see the other's point of view with tolerance for their convictions, even though they may be contrary to one's own; by trying to avoid judging the feelings of others, especially when involved with those whom one has once loved; by trying to overlook one's own failures as well as those of others because, even in a fall there is a hidden stepping-stone on which to rise above feelings of being either lower or higher than others in God's presence; by trying to attune oneself to the rhythm of all those whom one meets and in whose company there might be a hidden guidance, as there always is in everything which happens in one's life, providing one has lost oneself in the ecstasy of the 'Divine Presence.'

Extracts

The object of worship of the Sufi is beauty, the moral of the Sufi is harmony and the goal of the Sufi is love in all its aspects, human and divine.

The personality of the mystic, called in Sufi terms, *Aklak Allah* or 'divine manner,' is in the attunement of thought and action to the highest pitch of the soul. It is a manner free from pride, inspiring godliness in all expression.

To a question regarding the speculative theory of reincarnation, according to which reincarnation is repeated numerous times till reaching a stage of perfection, the Sufi response could be formulated as follows: When a seed is planted, after the blossoming of the plant, new seeds come forth and the same process repeats itself time and time again. The seed is always one of the same species, yet it is never the same seed which was originally planted and, what is more, each seed is also indirectly the source of innumerable others. Therefore, one could not call this process reincarnation of an individual seed.

Is one a machine or an engineer? If a machine, one then lingers on forever in mechanical irresponsibility. If an engineer, one becomes master of one's destiny, in which case one is responsible for any deeds that might weigh as heavy burdens on one's conscience.

Heaven and hell are the worlds of one's own conscience, and that which survives in the hereafter are those same worlds which we ourselves have created within ourselves here on this dense earth, where the laws of cause and effect are solid reality.

Why does one seek for happiness when happiness in reality is one's own being? One seeks because one is still under the illusion of the false self.

The Sufi understanding of the hereafter is best illustrated as being a gradual recognition of the illusory nature of all the experiences accumulated here on earth, through which the soul gains more and more clarity of consciousness, like a mirror upon which impressions have multiplied, yet the images have only reflected on its surface without engraving any permanent image, leaving the mirror of the soul immaculate and pure.

Behind the rose lies its past and, ever since the seeds were first produced, the heritage which the rose reflects in fragrance and colour has been preserved. Although there might be another flower in the same garden, under the same sun and in the same air, yet its fragrance and colour are different. In the same way, spirituality expresses itself in different ways and different terms, although all mystics are inspired by one and the same truth. It is lack of understanding of this ideal of unity which has given rise to religious differences, and these have been the cause of battles fought throughout the ages.

One often confuses truth with fact, but truth is of such a nature that it eventually uproots fact, which is often only illusion. If truth were so small as to be contained within the limitation of words, it could not be called truth.

All things appear different, depending on the angle from which they are considered, being only true to a certain extent in comparison to ultimate truth, which is beyond all speculative theory

When awakened from a dream, one might be sorry for not having known the end of the story and wish to go on dreaming. Similarly, in life, the intoxication of one's activities can be so enslaving that one easily overlooks their pointless nature.

Any role that we play as actor in the game of life soon becomes an intoxication. In that spell, one clings to the illusion of one's identification, even when realizing that one is the victim of a false image.

Whatever be one's condition, whether bright or gloomy, as soon as one discovers that nothing is really absolute, one recognizes that all is but a moment's game. All values are only worth what they are in comparison to others.

Good is not necessarily something which is stamped as such. Besides, that which is good at a certain time may be very wrong at another time, and that which one considers right could very well be considered wrong by another. Nevertheless, the main thing to consider in all cases is certainly to make every effort to act righteously according to one's own conscience.

Consciousness is a spark of intelligence and intelligence is the light of the soul itself. Therefore, the more the field of one's consciousness expands, the brighter the light and the broader becomes the outlook; whereas, the smaller the field of consciousness, the dimmer is the light and the shallower is one's insight

Consciousness is not tailored to a standard size of human thinking. Human thinking can expand to unlimited horizons. In other words, the mind occupies as much horizon of consciousness as one's thinking has expanded beyond the limitations of the self. This explains why the world can be as small as a lentil to one and, to another, it is as large as almighty space.

Gathekas 21

One cannot stop the natural course of life with either material or spiritual powers, just as one cannot hope to stop the rain because one is afraid of getting wet, but rather one could make use of an umbrella. In the same way, one cannot force others to act and think as one wishes, but one can certainly make every effort to first harmonize with oneself, so as to become an example for others who might be inspired thereby, rather than feeling compelled to act and think as one wishes them to. Simple hints can prove in time to have the effect of subtle messages which unfold into truth for the one whose insight is keen.

That which one wants to hide most are one's own faults. However, on the contrary, faults should not be hidden, but rather acknowledged if one has any real desire to be freed from them. By acknowledging one's faults one destroys them or finds a way to improve on them.

While climbing the mountain, if constantly delayed by useless problems, one might never reach the top. In the same way, in life, if one is constantly in strife over little things, one loses the opportunity of accomplishing great things. Therefore, one stays small and the other grows accordingly, and the higher one rises, the larger is the horizon.

Resignation of the self is the outcome of the soul's evolution. It is the path of love and wisdom—feeling great happiness in giving, offering all without expecting anything in return. However, resignation cannot be a virtue if it is offered out of helplessness, weakness or defeat, but only if it is the result of mastery over the self.

Conditions in life are not always mastered by conflict. If peace can be brought about, this is certainly preferable to a battle. The next step, however, is to rise above all that resulted in misunderstanding and useless conflict.

Whether one loves one's fellow humans or whether one loves God, when face to face with the sovereignty of love, all traces of the self as lover disappear in that light where there is neither 'mine' nor 'thine.'

Asceticism is certainly a means of developing inner realization and experiencing ecstasy, but of what use is *Samadhi* if one is not human in spirit? Balance in all things is the greatest responsibility in the life of a mystic.

Some are deeply moved by beauty in music, poetry and art, whereas others are as dull as stone if something subtle is not yet awakened in their hearts. Just as smoke obscures the brightness of the flame, in the same manner the light of the soul is dulled by the consciousness of 'I.'

One judges others on grounds of that which one thinks as being right or wrong, not realizing that one's judgement is based on that which one has learned from others, and that what is wrong for one person could very well be right for another. Besides, that which might be right at one time, might be wrong at another time and, what is more, one's insight can change day by day in accordance with one's spiritual development.

Seven Aspects of Brotherhood and Sisterhood

From a human point of view:
talking to each other in his or her own tone.

From a social point of view:
showing understanding for the opinions of others.

From a religious point of view:
promoting the unity of religious ideals.

From a moral point of view: offering all that is expected of one while expecting nothing in return.

From a point of view of wisdom:
being a living example of love, harmony and beauty.

From a mystical point of view:
freeing oneself from the illusion of the self.

From a spiritual point of view:
attuning oneself and others to the divine 'Spirit of Guidance.'

Gathas

I. Superstitions, Customs and Beliefs
   Etekad, Rasm U Ravaj

II. Insight
   Kashf

III. Symbology
   Nakshi Bandi

IV. Breath
   Pasi Anfas

V. Morals
   Saluk

VI. Everyday Life
   Taqwa Taharat

VII. Metaphysics
   Tasawwuf

I. Superstitions, Customs and Beliefs
Etekad, Rasm U Ravaj

Beliefs and Superstitions

The term belief is used when referring to an idea or an ideal which one respects, recognizing the wisdom which has inspired it. However, following a belief from fear of the consequences of not acting in accordance with rules, is what could be called being superstitious.

Various cultures have their own beliefs and superstitions. Some of these descend from ancestral intuitive sources, while others are psychological impulses which grow in time into customs and habits, becoming thereby part of the identity of a specific culture. Nevertheless, there is always some wisdom hidden in every belief, and it is only out of ignorance that a person says, "That is not my belief." Such a statement only reveals one's own inability to understand another person's point of view.

In fact, one often confuses belief with truth when, through lack of understanding of one's own belief, one ignores all other beliefs and holds one's own to be the only truth. Such a belief nails one to the ground, rather than helping one to fly up into higher spheres.

Greeting Customs

Among numerous customs existing in various parts of the world some are very much alike and others very different, especially those relating to physical expressions such as greetings, signs of respect and psychological insight.

The Hindus greet by joining the palms of the hands, symbolizing perfection in the meeting of the powers of *ida* and *pingala* (the active and receptive channels). The statue of Buddha, sitting cross-legged with hands joined and eyes closed, also symbolizes perfection. The Chinese greet each other by clasping the hands and then touching each other's clasped hands, symbolizing by this exchange that same concept of the power of perfection. The Arabs shake both hands together symbolizing fullness in the exchange of that same power. The Persians press one hand to the heart, suggesting being united wholeheartedly with the 'Divine Presence.' The western custom of kissing both cheeks also symbolizes an exchange of *prana* on both sides (*ida* and *pingala*).

The custom of kissing the hand reveals deepest fondness and respect. The Hindu custom of touching the feet of a holy person symbolizes seeking contact with the rays of magnetism which are the easiest to reach, before receiving the blessing which follows. In daily life, magnetism is exchanged when shaking hands with others, and at that moment, the weaker one receives positive vibrations from the stronger one. When rising to welcome a visitor or walking toward that person, one is building up magnetism in order to be in a position to attune one's vibrations to those of the visitor, as well as preparing oneself psychologically. Bowing the head indicates thoughtfulness, whereas keeping the head erect when greeting indicates thoughtlessness. Waving to a parting visitor expresses one's good thoughts and appreciation.

The Hanuman Idol

In India there is a custom of offering oil to the idol of Hanuman, the monkey-king. Hanuman is suggestive of man's primitive nature, and in pouring oil on that idol, there is a secret reminder of the idea of softening one's own character.

At the occasion of weddings among the Hindus, maidens anoint the head, shoulders, arms, hands, knees and feet of the bride and bridegroom. As oil signifies softness, the custom gives a psychological reminder of the idea of becoming docile toward one another when entering into married life. The great lesson to be learned from this is to soften one's words, actions, thoughts and feelings, as symbolized in the custom of standing humbly, face to face with the idol of Hanuman, whose crudeness is vanquished when one battles against that tendency in one's own character.

Bells and Gongs

The origin of gongs and bells ringing in churches, temples and pagodas is to be found in the old tradition, known to the Hindus as Mantra Yoga. Although the usual explanation given for the ringing of gongs and bells is that these are used in a call for prayer, nevertheless, mystical insight into this tradition sees it as an attunement of the heart of the worshipper to that heavenly resonance which resounds in the sounds of the bells and gongs. Gongs re-echoing to the divine source, from which all tones derive, bring spiritual intoxication to the listener. The mystical secret of the intoxicating power of sound has been abundantly described by ancient Sufis in their poetic references to the 'Bowl of Saki.' This term is used to refer to the human heart, in which there is only room for one—either the 'I' or the wine of intoxication, which creates the illusion of an empty bowl which will never feel full unless conscious of the 'Divine Presence' which stands ever within.

Customs in a House of Worship

Flowers symbolize beauty and, in this, the feeling of response. Flowers also reveal the great magic of colour as well as communicating their secret perfumes, which rise through the breath, penetrating right into the feeling heart, just as incense does. Beauty, colour and perfume combined with the mystical power of sound, experienced in singing and chanting, awakens the spirit of the worshippers who are thereby enabled to fully respond inwardly to the atmosphere of the religious offering.

Custom of Covering the Head and Veiling the Face

This custom is mistakenly associated with the teachings of the Prophet Mohammed. If one can trace any connection between the Prophet and this custom, which developed much later in the East, there are only two known historical incidents in the Prophet's life time. One incident occurred when peasant women, dancing in improper clothing were told to dress more decently. The other incident was when the ladies of the Prophet's household were advised to cover their faces in response to their dislike of the sight of the horrors on the battlefield.

In the East, aged women and widows cover their heads to hide their grief and emotions. Brides veil their faces as a symbolical protection from the evil eye of jealousy and envy, and even from the admiration of the guests at the wedding. Of course, from a mystical point of view, this is a sign of modesty, treasuring the gift of beauty and keeping sober amidst turmoil and excitement. Every outgoing activity, such as looking, breathing and speaking, robs one of one's magnetism, which the mystic tries to preserve. Even hairs are like channels of radiance and this also explains the origin of various customs of covering the head, signifying the preservation of magnetism, the head being the superior part of the body.

Custom of Seclusion of Women in the East

Woman being more impressionable than man, the task of woman as mother is so much more delicate than that of the father. With her thoughts and feelings, the mother moulds the character of the coming child, and being particularly impressionable during pregnancy, her emotions are that much more intense and reach directly into the depth of her being, re-echoing upon the very soul of the child in formation.

From the moment that the child opens its eyes, it seeks the protection of the mother. Womanhood, whether as mother, sister, daughter, friend or wife is, in every form of relationship, the source of man's happiness, this being at the same time the secret of woman's happiness. If such customs as seclusion of women in the East ever came into being, it was originally done with the noble intention of offering love and protection to womanhood.

The Phrase in the Bible, "Eat my Flesh and Drink my Blood"

In these words, 'flesh' symbolizes the knowledge of God, which can be described as conviction and strength; whereas 'blood' symbolizes God's love, which can be described as expression and movement. "Eat the flesh," can be understood as meaning, "Absorb the knowledge of God." "Drink the blood," can be understood as meaning, "Let the love of God penetrate your entire being."

The Horse, Symbol of the Power of Mind

When the mind is under control it is like a well-trained horse. When the mind is uncontrolled it is like a restless horse. There are many historical legends involving the horse, such as the one about Lahu (son of Rama) running in pursuit of the horse Kalanki; the story of Krishna, as charioteer for Arjuna, narrated in the Mahabharata; and the holy exploits of the Islamic heroes, Hassan and Hussein with their sacred horse Duldul. All these highly religious and moral lessons are precious descriptions of the horse as a symbol of the mind power.

The Greek Mysteries

The little that is really known about Greek Mysteries has been interpreted in various ways. Some suppose Greek Mysteries to have been a course in agriculture *(Ziraat)* taught in strict secrecy (hence the mystery), and to be initiated meant to be made silent. Others understand Greek Mysteries to have been esoteric schools, perhaps the inspiration of the ancient Sufis.

Prior to initiation in the mysteries, the preparation was extremely severe with various hardships to be overcome as well as tests with the elements: earth, water, fire, air. After these experiences a glorious light was seen as an awakening from all material limitations.

In the temples, the gods were worshipped and music played an important role. Here we find a strong parallel with 'the mystery of gods,' called *Ilmi Rabbli* by the ancient Persian Sufis, meaning the attributes of the one God. Later these were known by Sufis as *wazifas*, which are now practised in all Sufi schools. The music played in the Greek temples as a means of spiritual development is now practised, especially in the *Chistia* esoteric schools, by the *Qawalis*, in mystical meetings called *Sama,* in an attempt to awaken the deepest emotions, which is the very secret of all revelation.

The Shadow, Shudra

An ancient Hindu custom which is nowadays considered to be a superstition, consisted of not allowing the shadow of a person thought to be unholy or unlucky to fall upon oneself, a pregnant woman, a new-born child, the shrine in one's home or the food or other essentials.

The vibration of a person crossing one's path can have a powerful influence on the wheel of life, turning it to the right if atmosphere of the person is positive compared to one's own, or regrettably to the left when the life-giving rays of the radiant sun are veiled by the cold darkness of the shadow, *Shudra*.

Often innocent souls, lacking a positive nature, become victims of undesirable personalities who stand in their way, obscuring the light for which they crave. The more one becomes conscious of the shadow of *Shudra* crossing one's path, the better one understands the secret behind this custom of protecting oneself from the effect of the evil eye.

Omens

The influence of an impression can have a strong effect upon an initiative, particularly when the impression is received at the beginning of the undertaking. This is what is understood by the words 'good omen' and 'bad omen,' now considered by some to be plain superstitions.

Nevertheless, it is a fact that, when planning a project, the sight of prosperous accomplishments influences the mind with positive impressions, whereas the sight of unsuccessful undertakings influences the mind with negative impressions, which in either case affect one's projects accordingly.

Furthermore, for purely psychological reasons, it is advisable to avoid asking such questions as, "Why? When? Where?" of a person who is fully concentrated on a project. Such questions stand in the way of the ongoing stream of thought and have the effect of cutting that stream, as do negative impressions crossing one's path while on the way to success.

The Importance of Time and Planetary Influences

The influence of the sun and moon have in all ages been considered with great interest. The sun represents divine light and the moon, the human heart. When the forces of the divine light and the human heart join during the waxing of the moon, it is like drawing power within. In harmony with nature's tides, this is the most appropriate time to accomplish projects.

In the middle of the night, between the old day and the new, the *kemal* atmosphere offers perfect stillness. The *kemal* vibrations are also there when the sun is at the zenith, but without the quiet stillness of midnight.

Time has influences upon the weather, the sea, the trees, plants and flowers, so it also has influences upon all living creatures, although we may appear to be most independent of its effects upon our affairs in life.

The entire cosmos is based upon a certain rhythm which affects the planetary systems as well as all individuals, and this rhythm works as a hidden law which governs the action of the entire universe but remains unseen.

II. Insight
Kashf

The Mind as Mirror

The soul uses instruments through which the consciousness becomes aware of various experiences—seeing through the eyes, for example, hearing through the ears, tasting through the tongue, not to mention the senses of smell and touch. However, between the soul and the senses, the mind is the central mirror of consciousness, receiving impressions through the senses and reflecting them upon the soul. In this connection, the brain, like the rest of the body, is the instrument of the mind, just as the mind is the instrument of the soul. Although these instruments are at the service of the soul, offering the structures and appearances of knowledge, in doing so they are also limiting the freedom of the soul.

In the same way in which the sight can be either focused or open to all impressions (and may be conditioned by far or nearsightedness), the mind as an instrument of the soul, can focus upon another mind, receiving thereby impressions of all its contents. However, when the mind ventures to experience life through the limited channels of the body, the horizon of its perception is thereby constricted by the degree of specialization of the five senses. Unfortunately, mankind usually attaches too much importance to using the various functions of the body as instruments of the mind, seldom allowing the mind to function freely beyond the limitations of physical existence. Similarly, when the horizon of the soul is limited to the vision through the mind, its openness onto the infinite is, of course, restricted to the concept of individuality.

Since it is difficult for the mind to perceive life independently of the body, it is clearly that much more difficult for the soul to perceive life independently of the mind. Therefore, the esoteric training of the Sufis consists in developing in the mind a certain independence from the body; and, for the soul, a certain independence from the mind. In order to accomplish this, several concentration practices (called *safa*) are given, which have as effect, the effacing of the impressions of the external physical garb from the awareness of the mind, and effacing the mind consciousness from the mirror of the soul.

Gathas II 33

Aspects of Knowledge

Three aspects of knowledge exist—the knower, the known, and the knowing, or in other words, the seer, the seen and the faculty of seeing. When the illusion separating these three aspects is dispelled, the mystic then sees one and the same reality in these three different concepts. It is this concept which the Christians call 'Trinity' and the Hindus call *Trimurti*, symbolized by a three-pronged fork.

In that which the seer sees, is the seer's own light. The first lesson that the mystic learns is the relationship between oneself and that which one sees. The ancient Vedantists adopted this lesson, which is understood by the words *Tat Twam Asi*, meaning "As Thou art, so am I." When seeing from this point of view, the inner sight becomes clear.

Usually there are barriers separating persons from each other, such as jealousy, prejudice, dislike and many other causes of separation. But why do people not understand each other? It is because they do not always understand that it is they, who ask themselves that question, who are the cause of the barriers which separate them from one another. For a saintly person there are no barriers distancing one from others. As a result of contemplation upon God, the point of view of 'I' has been effaced and the idea of duality is no longer in the way. Thus, the seer is aware of the light of the soul, which radiates in all that is seen.

The Glance

The glance of the seer has several characteristics, one being the power of observation; another, the power of clarifying; and a third characteristic, the awakening of positive qualities in another.

It is possible to turn a friend into an enemy just by thinking that he or she is so, as it is also possible to change an enemy into a friend just by expecting him or her to become so. In the same manner, the mystic has the power to give a positive turn to everything in which he or she is involved, such as turning ugliness into beauty. Consequently, a deep thinker realizes that things need not always be as they appear to be; it is we who make them appear to be as such. One's entire life could be one of ugliness, or could be shaped into a vision of sublime beauty. The lord of the yogis, Shiva, is pictured with a cobra around his neck, symbolizing death, the appearance of which frightens everyone——but for Shiva, it was a symbol of life. This suggests that a symbol of death could illustrate life, if one wished to see it as such, the reaction in any case, arising from the point of view.

The first characteristic of the glance, the power of observation, is the outcome of clarity of vision. The second, clarifying power, is the outcome of inner illumination. The third characteristic, awakening of positive qualities, is the consequence of consciousness opened upon the inner self, known by the term *iman*.

Physiognomy

The study of physiognomy can be deepened with the help of intuition. The first stage in this study is one of observation, which opens up two points of view—the analytical, meaning the understanding of each characteristic individually, and the synthetic, meaning the understanding of harmony when all individual parts function together.

The more one observes human characteristics from these two points of view, the more one marvels at the wonders of creation, behind all of which one then sees divine evidence. Every part of a human being reveals the individual's past, present and future. This can be explained by considering that every impulse creates vibrations, which radiate in different directions. Some vibrations influence the beating of the physical heart and thereby the blood-circulation. Others influence the thought, becoming thereby readable in the expression of the face, the behaviour, the attitude and the condition of the feeling heart.

Gathas II 35

The Meaning of Movements

One is not always conscious of one's movements, yet every movement that one makes does communicate some meaning. The seer recognizes that every movement arises from some cause and, on the other hand, every movement has a consequence. Therefore, in the movements, the nature of a person can be discovered. Crookedness in nature results in crookedness of gestures. Grace in movement suggests beauty in the nature, whereas lack of grace suggests lack of harmony. Rhythm of movements suggests balance, and lack of rhythm suggests lack of balance. Also the predominance of the five elements can be recognized in the actions of sitting, walking, lying, laughing and crying.

Every movement denotes a certain thought and feeling, for in every thought and feeling the waves of the mind, so to speak, rise and fall like the sea, which may be either rough or calm. Some movements suggest various states of mind. For instance, wrath, revenge, conceit and pride are expressed in upward movements, while downward movements show depression, helplessness, meekness and submission. Movements to the right can imply struggle and power, and movement toward the left can imply art and skill. Contraction of all sorts suggests fear, coldness, or indifference, whereas stretching tendencies suggest action, strength and power. The tendency of turning without reason denotes confusion, while the tendency to pinch and press shows uneasiness of mind. Stillness without stiffness expresses calm and peace.

Facial Expressions

The attitude of the mind is also seen in subtle changes in the features of the face such as slight movements of the eyes, lips, eyebrows and head, which are expressive of thoughts and feelings. When the eyebrows turn upward, this denotes an egotistical tendency and shrewdness. The puckering of the lips denotes humorous tendencies. Restlessness in the eyes denotes confusion, whereas glancing sideways, either right or left, denotes cleverness.

One's expression is even more indicative of one's nature and character than is the shape of one's features. All states of mind, such as weakness, fear, happiness, joy, love, hatred, strength and power, appear as an open book to someone with insight. As there are different types of sight, such as long and short sight, in the same manner there are different types of minds—minds which only reach a certain distance and no further, and others that reach further. In the same way, one person only sees the outer action of a person, whereas another sees the reason behind the action. These abilities cannot be explained, they can only be experienced.

Observation and Concentration

The faculty of seeing 'the cause behind the cause' can be developed through observation, whereas focusing the mind upon an object is what is understood by concentration. Keenness of observation is a phenomenon in itself. The person whose sight is not steady cannot observe fully and, in the same way, the mind which is not steady does not have the capacity of observing fully. Therefore, the self-mastered person develops full control over body and mind, thereby having balance in all things. Wisdom is the outcome of outward steadiness and insight into the inner world. Every object is a vibration, which could be understood as spirit. In ancient times, the seers recognized the spirit of all things, the spirit of mountains, trees, stars, planets, rivers, lakes, pools and seas. No doubt it is easier to have contact with the spirit of mankind, rather than with the vibration of objects, for the very reason that the human being is the most living of all creatures in the universe.

III. Symbology
Nakshi Bandi

Symbols

Wisdom has been expressed all down the ages in different ways and forms appropriate to the time, offering modes of inner awakening through symbols, by the means of which, the veils of truth are carefully unravelled, disclosing beauty which words are inadequate to reveal. In all religions, even as far back in history as ancient Greece and Egypt, symbols have been the predominant vehicles of truth, as well as its protection. Regrettably, those who do not understand the secret language of symbols have opposed these violently, especially in the Islamic period and during the Reformation.

Symbols reveal much relating to human nature and to godly attributes as well, indicating paths leading to the divine ideal. There is joy in understanding deeper subjects which do not necessarily find place in the average mode of thinking, this understanding requiring intuition and deep insight. The sacred symbol is a language in itself which speaks without words, writes without writing and is, in so doing, a secret means of preservation of the beauty of truth for ages and ages.

The Symbol of the Sun

Light has always offered the greatest attraction in all its different aspects such as fire, jewels and all that shines and is bright. Yet the cosmos has a still greater attraction, which one feels when contemplating the sun and the stars beyond. All this shining light inspired the devotees of long ago to worship the sun as a symbol of the 'All-pervading.' This symbol of God is pictured in various forms and images in Persia, China, Japan, Egypt and Greece. Furthermore, in all religions, the 'Bringer of the Message' is pictured with a golden disc above the head, which also suggests the light of the sun. The golden disc, also called *Zardash* (which is the origin of the name 'Zarathustra') was later pictured above the heads of kings in Persia. This same symbol is also related to saints and angels in the Christian faith, and to different images in Hindu and Buddhist temples.

A deeper insight into the image of the sun reveals four lines forming a cross. The symbol of the cross existed among the Brahmins ages before the coming of the Christ. This same symbol is also at the origin of the two sacred symbols called *Chakra* and *Trishul*. Strangely enough the written words for 'sun' in both Arabic and Persian illustrate the shape of the sun, although symbols are forbidden in Islam.

The symbol of the cross contains in itself the essence of all geometrical shapes, besides being an equation which satisfies all possible interpretations. When seen as a picture of life, the vertical line of the cross illustrates activity, whereas the horizontal line denotes obstruction and limitation. When related to the life of Christ, the cross signifies crucifixion of the self on the path of truth, effacing the concept of 'I am' and replacing it with 'Thou art,' whereby the veil that hides the 'Divine Presence' is removed. The symbol of the cross not only pictures pain and suffering, but also depicts the path of self-denial, which is the sacrifice that the seeker on the inner path is confronted with when possessed by truth, a sacrifice which is followed by resurrection. Nevertheless, for those who can see through symbols, both crucifixion and resurrection are illusions, known by the ancient Hindus as *maya* or *mithya*, a Sanskrit word which is the root of the word 'myth'.

The Egyptian Symbol

Egyptian symbolism is one of the most ancient forms of worship, from which many other forms of worship have been inspired and elaborated upon in numberless varieties of images, illustrating deepest esoteric teachings. The Egyptian symbol of a golden disc (the sun symbol) flanked by two wings and two snakes on the right and on the left, symbolically represents the three powers of the spirit: the sound of the universe, the colour of the five elements and the energy of action. The golden disc in the centre symbolizes the 'light of the spirit' which, like the physical light of the sun, contains all the colours of the rainbow. These colours are also present in the five elements, each one characterizing those specific vibrations which are at the origin of the energy of such actions as spreading (earth), flowing (water), rising (fire), turbulence (air), and withdrawal into serenity (ether).

These same vibrations, understood in another way, constitute sound, which is the very source of all manifestation. The two snakes symbolize the directions taken in life by the spirit, either a receptive one or a creative one. This idea is also found in the Hindu philosophy of the *kundalini* energy with its two complementary directions called *ida* and *pingala,* which the Sufis know as *jelal* and *jemal*. The mystics also call these directions 'the sun influence' and 'the moon influence,' manifesting their energies either on the right side of the body or on the left side, when flowing through the right nostril or the left one, respectively.

The secret of all success resides in the appropriate use of these energies, in harmony with the type of activity in which one is involved. This knowledge is what is indicated by the term 'esotericism.' Esotericism is a knowledge which reveals to the seeker after truth the great power of the spirit, so that one is constantly aware of the spirit within, reminding one that one is not only a physical body, not only an earthly creature, but that one also belongs to heaven.

The Symbol of the Flying Dove

The dove, an inhabitant of the skies, pictures the soul, which dwells above while at the same time being dependent upon the laws of the earth. It therefore symbolizes the personality of those spiritual beings whose dwelling place is both heaven and earth. The symbol of the dove illustrates most beautifully the personality of the 'Bringer of the Message' who, while focusing steadily upon the heavens above, whither the return journey is the constant cry of the heart, journeys from time to time all through the ages, to this world of sorrow and disappointment, where life is subject to love and hatred, praise and blame. In the fulfillment of God's message to humanity, the 'Bringer of the Message' is never really separated from the divine origin, even amidst the commitments and limitations of human attachments experienced throughout the flight from heaven to earth and from earth to heaven in answer to the call.

The Symbol of the Sufi Movement

The heart with wings on either side signifies the human heart situated between the physical body (matter) and the soul (spirit). When the soul is focused upon the material plane, its love is shown in earthly longings, whereas when focused on the higher spheres it is attracted to spiritual bliss. This upward flight is seen in the image of the flying heart, which the ancient Egyptian esoteric schools used as a symbol of the path toward spiritual attainment. The crescent moon, which receives the light of the sun and increases thereby until it is full, symbolizes receptivity in the human heart to the light of God.

The five-pointed star represents the ever-radiant divine light of the 'Spirit of Guidance.' In other words, the symbol offers the message that the human heart is liberated from the limitations of the self when responding to the divine light within.

Geometrical Symbols

Every mystic and every artist knows the value of the vertical and horizontal line, which form the skeleton of every form. Geometrical symbols such as the dot, the circle, the pyramid and many others also carry a mystical and artistic significance insofar as we direct our consciousness to the secret power which is latent in line and shape, and which can produce great effects on both the observer and the environment.

The dot is the essence of all figures, for in the extension of the dot resides the source of every line. Obviously, the extension in either direction, horizontal or vertical, determines the angle and orientation of every form, be it up or down, to the right or the left. In Sanskrit, the dot is called *bindu*, which means source and origin of all creation. Paradoxically, however, in mathematics the dot also means zero or nothing. The dot is, therefore, nothing and everything at the same time, expressing the mystical idea that everything there is, is everything and nothing at the same time. The dot can also develop into the circle, in which there is infinite movement or perpetual motion, and therefore the dot is a symbol of the entire manifested universe.

The triangle symbolizes the beginning, the continuation and the end. It is the sign of life seen in three aspects. From this originated the symbol of the 'Trinity,' known by the Hindus as *Trimurti*, meaning Brahma, Vishnu and Shiva (the creator, the sustainer and the destroyer). Later, it was known by the Christians as the Father, the Son and the Holy Ghost.

The Symbol of the Mushroom

The Chinese philosopher is shown holding a mushroom stem, symbolically illustrating the idea of holding and controlling earthly matter. Another meaning to this symbol is a reminder that the sage is expected to be gentle, refined and humble like a mushroom. This symbol also teaches that all that comes from the earth, however precious it might appear to be, is of no more value than a mushroom, which may be destroyed at any moment. At the same time, this symbol shows the independence and indifference of the mystic, for the mushroom is independent of any care whatsoever. All other plants respond to rain and storm and make a noise, but the mushroom stands still. In the same way, the soul of the mystic is trained, in silence, to be free from all the storms of life that pull one back on the way, achieving thereby, in silence, the inner experience of the awakening of the soul.

The Symbol of the Shoe

A Chinese picture of a sage holding one shoe in his hand while the other is on his foot, is a symbolical illustration of life after death. This picture signifies that the change which comes after death is just as unimportant as taking off one shoe. In this picture, the body represents the self, the one shoe left on the foot represents the mind which lives on after death, and the act of taking off the other shoe represents the withdrawal of the soul from the body. This picture suggests the realization of the hereafter while still on earth, illustrating the nothingness of this material existence and the smallness of this physical condition in comparison with the greatness of the soul.

The Symbol of Carrying Peaches

A Chinese picture of a sage carrying peaches on the shoulder suggests that the object of life is first of all to be fruitful. Whether or not one is spiritual, if one's life is not fruitful one has not fulfilled life's purpose, which is not only to bear fruit for oneself but also for others. If life were only meant for the purpose of spirituality, it would be better not to have been born, since the soul is itself all spirituality that there is. The entire creation is greater than righteousness or spirituality, which are by themselves only the means, not the goal. If there is a goal at all, it is fruitfulness. Fruitfulness is to be understood in three ways: having the benefit of one's own success, then benefiting from profitable circumstances in which one is involved and, finally, benefiting in one's own merits and also helping others to profit from these, this being the utmost fulfillment of our life.

The Symbol of the Dragon

The most characteristic Chinese symbol is certainly the dragon which illustrates both eternal life and death, in the sense of a change from mortality to eternity. Sometimes the Chinese dragon is given the appearance of a tiger, a seal, a snake with wings or even a human shape, meaning that life can be manifested in many forms. The dragon suggests the concept of mortality which is always present. It is also a reminder of the constant obstacles experienced on the way to eternity and which can be vanquished when conquering the dragon, the ego or lower self, which is the cause of all differences with others. The dragon, despite all its material power, can be overpowered by the spirit, which is the hidden lesson behind this symbol.

Water and Wine

In the Vedanta and the Old Testament, water symbolizes the spirit because water gives life to the earth by its very nature, as spirit gives life to all creatures. Just as water mixes with earth, so spirit mixes with matter, giving it life and movement, but at the same time spirit remains abstracted from matter, just as water rises above the sinking earth.

Wine, which is considered in some religions to be a sacred symbol, has inspired various images in ancient cultures. Among the Hindus, the image of Shiva is connected to the sacredness of divine intoxication. In the Zoroastrian tradition, there is the story of Jamshed drinking out of the *Yima Jamshed*, the 'divine bowl'. In Islam, the holy fountain *Kauzu 'l-Kausar* is a sacred fountain of intoxication. In the Christian religion, wine symbolizes the blood of Christ.

Wine, which is produced from the annihilation of grapes, losing their individuality though not the real essence, while changing into a different condition, illustrates so beautifully the mystical idea of losing the false self, and in this true sacrament the real self is born again.

The Symbol of the Curl of the Beloved

In the Sufi literature of Persia, reference is made to the 'curl of the beloved.' This curl signifies wisdom in its finest form, where perfect, unlimited truth has been carefully adjusted to circumstances so that it becomes ornament and thereby intelligible and tangible to the limited understanding of humanity. Truth is divine and by interpreting it at the level of human understanding, beauty is added to it, which is illustrated by the image of the beloved's curl.

When contemplating and observing nature in all its aspects one discovers perfect wisdom behind inexplicable puzzles, which represent outward responses to divine impulse. Another lesson to be learned from the symbol of the curl is that wisdom can neither be defined nor explained, just as the length and breadth of the beloved's curl cannot explain the depth of our love for the beloved.

IV. Breath
Pasi Anfas

The Science of Breath

In the East mysticism is understood as being the knowledge of the science of breath. Whether they be Buddhists, Vedantists or Sufis, all recognized this science as being the first and last lesson on the path of spirituality. A mystic is able to project *prana* to any part of the body, charging that part with radiance and magnetism. However, that phenomena only occurs when the breath has been developed and accordingly purified. The most beautiful music does not sound right on an untuned instrument. Breath is a channel through which all expressions from within are communicated. It is the magnetic current running between the everlasting and the mortal condition. All intuition, inspiration and even miraculous powers are experienced through the magic action of the breath.

The power of the breath, called *kundalini* by the Hindus, circulates within the spine along basic channels or *nadis*. This most important subject is incorrectly disregarded by some who imagine that distress might be the result of opening up the *chakras* through the use of breathing exercises. It is like saying that the eyes of a child should never be opened to reality for fear of being exposed to temptations. All virtue lies in self-control, not in ignorance. Life is only really worthwhile if it is lived fully.

Rhythm in Breath

Breath is the central theme to be considered in life since the breath governs the entire physical and mental mechanism of our being. Along with the importance of the purity of the breath channels, rhythm in breath is the magic key which can unlock all the treasures which the breath can offer. Rhythm is a natural tendency which is seen in all creation. No atom would move if it were not subject to the laws of rhythm. Orderliness in one's life is a sign of rhythm. When the rhythm of the breath is in disorder, all things go wrong and one shows an appearance of an unbalanced state, either physical or mental, or both.

Breath is our life. It is the breath which holds all the particles of our being together. Therefore, when this power fails, there is also a disturbance in our control over the various particles of our being. When the breath is in order, it has a revivifying function, absorbing out of space both spirit and substance required for our well being, while purifying us of all that is undesirable. When there is irregularity in the rhythm of breath or deficiencies in the breathing organs, or the influence of noxious substances which pollute the breath flow, the entire mechanism is put out of balance.

Breath is the medium through which the outer life and the life within are connected. Through the channel of breath all elements that the body requires are absorbed, as well as the subtle vibrations of *prana*, which the mind receives in the form of intuition, inspiration and magnetism. It is also with the help of breath that negative thought-waves and undesirable elements which have been absorbed can be neutralized.

When a breathing exercise is given, it is above all the rhythm in that practice which is meant to be observed, and not only the breathing. The breathing is another aspect of the exercise. It can be either very dense (called *kasif* by the Sufis) or fine (called *latif* by the Sufis). The dense breath is used when making physical effort, whereas the fine breath is that which penetrates through all the *chakras* and the finest channels, reaching the innermost parts of our being.

Fikar

Once one becomes conscious of the natural rhythm in the breath, which is like the movements of a swing, one can then add to it a chosen thought, expressed in a word mentally repeated with each inhalation and exhalation. This is called *Fikar* by the Sufis. The one who has not gained power over the breath is like a monarch who has no authority over the nation. However, even when the techniques of contraction (holding in or out) and of expansion (the exhalation) have been developed, all is still of no avail unless one knows what to absorb from the incoming breath and what to expel in the outgoing breath.

This explains why it is so important to really know something about the working of *Fikar* which, when practised for some years, not only helps to regulate the rhythm of the breath (and in so doing insures an appropriate blood circulation with all the positive advantages related to health in general), but also helps to develop concentration and thereby memory, as well as the ability to free one's mind from undesirable thoughts and feelings.

The more length and breadth (or capacity) in the breath, the more resource there is for creative thought. Length in breath denotes length in life. Some who have much volume in their breath may lack length in the exhalation. Others might have length in the exhalation, but might lack capacity in the inhalation. It is the harmonious proportion of length and capacity which brings about the perfect balance in the breath and thereby, also, physical and mental balance.

Breath and Light

When the breath is developed, becoming so-to-speak a magnetic current of higher consciousness, it is then projected as rays of light which are perceptible as colours, corresponding to the different proportions of the five elements manifesting in the exhalation. These rays fall upon the screen of the mind like the beams of a search light, helping the mind to see in all clarity the object of thought, which took form originally from the magnetic currents of the *prana* in breath, manifesting its radiance through the five senses.

The qualities of intuition and inspiration are consequently dependent upon the intensity of those rays of light shining upon the mind, and the ability of the breath to channel the inner call to the organs of expression.

It is the subtle vibrations of the breath which could be called thought-waves, transmitting thought from one mind to another as if two mirrors were placed facing each other. In experiences such as mind reading, it is the overlapping of the breath vibrations of one and the other which explains this phenomena.

It is the light in the breath and the intensity of the vibrations of the elements therein, which is understood from the term 'aura.' This explains why the Hindus call breath *prana*, which means 'the light from within which has become exteriorized.' This light is brought about when connecting the *jelal* and *jemal* forces at a mystical level of consciousness, just as the light in a lamp only manifests when the positive and negative currents are appropriately connected. The vibrations of breath are the substance of all expression. The spoken word strikes upon the heart like a hammer on a gong, but the power of breath strikes even without the word. The breath of a spiritual person, which communicates love and sympathy, is vitalizing. It is not an exaggeration to say that the phenomena of life and its mysteries are all to be found in the science of breath which, when mastered, offers great blessing and happiness.

V. Morals
Saluk

Divine Presence

For a Sufi, God is not only a heavenly ideal, but God is also a friend, a beloved, with whom one's dealings are as with lover and beloved. This explains why all praise is offered to God in thought of the wonders of creation and, when dealing with one's fellow human, all actions of kindness and consideration are done as though these are being offered to God. However, the wise take care not to pride themselves upon their good deeds, keeping in mind that vanity is a veil which hides the presence of God from sight; whereas love for God in the absence of the self, results in the expansion of the heart, in the light whereof every action becomes a virtue.

If God is love and if love is sacred, one avoids degrading the values of that sacredness through vain utterances. Love is in itself a revelation, for which no study, no concentration, no meditation and no piety is required, when once a spark has been kindled. Seeking for spirituality without love is a vain search because, if spirituality is to be found anywhere it is in the heart, once that kindling spark has grown into a glowing flame, throwing light upon the dark path of the 'false ego.'

Under the fascination of worldly powers, one overlooks the greatness of one's own inner powers, which can be discovered when the 'I' is replaced by 'Thou art.' However, self-denial does not mean renouncing life's duties nor nature's sources of happiness. Self-denial means to deny that little self, which creeps in at every possible occasion to eclipse the bright light of the 'Divine Presence.' In self-denial, happiness is more intensely appreciated because one has risen above the notion of wanting, while respecting one's duties toward the accomplishment of the purpose of one's life, which is in truth only an infinitely small part of all creation.

The Nature of Happiness

Happiness, which is clearly the longing of every soul, reveals its secret in the knowledge of the 'true self.' In humans, this knowledge is forgotten from the first day when, at the moment of birth, the soul was moulded into shape and found itself caught in the net of the 'false self.' Happiness means making the right use of those means which have been granted, for the purpose of accomplishing the duties that are expected of us. Unfortunately, our vision of right and wrong is not always correct, nor does it always correspond to the vision of others. Happiness means understanding the wants and needs of our physical body, discovering the many mysteries of the mind, and seeking enlightenment of the spirit.

How few realize that the heart is like a dome, within which all is re-echoed, whether good or bad, creating thereby either uplifting or disturbing influences that become in time the characteristics of one's own personality. The mastery over all impulses is portrayed by the Hindus as a dance at the 'Court of Indra,' and every movement of the dance is offered to the 'Divine Presence.' That art which the Sufis call the 'Art of Personality,' resides in polishing the rough edges of one's vanity, since vanity is, in fact, the hidden source from which both virtue and sin arise in one way or other. It is in the practice of this art that the character is ennobled.

The Art of Personality

The 'Art of Personality' is like the art of music, wherein ear and voice training are indispensable in discerning the pitch of a tone and its interval from another, for the purpose of establishing harmony. When relating this same ideal of harmony to our fellow humans, it is clear that the beauty of the personality shines out in such tendencies as a friendly attitude in word and action, spontaneity in the art of offering one's love without any expectation of return, and in the awakening of the true sense of justice, all of which are the expressions of the music of the personality.

The 'Art of Personality' is a precious secret in one's life. This art is manifested in all feelings for beauty and for sincerity, in thought, speech and action. It is revealed in a considerate attitude toward others, and in being aware of the re-echo of all that one does in life, and for which one shall have to account sooner or later.

A human being cannot excuse a negative behaviour saying, "I was only born as a thorn, so how could I be a rose?" for unlike a plant, we are all granted the gift of free will. The beauty, fragrance and colour latent in the root are expressed in the rose rather than in the thorn, although rose and thorn are both part of the same plant and have the same root. In the same way, the angelic qualities latent in the human being, can be revealed in the beauty and charm of the personality, not withstanding one's human origin.

The charm of the personality, which is expressed in beauty, is also deeply felt in the tone of sincerity. The secret of this art resides in a perfect balance between these elements of beauty and sincerity, since a polished manner without sincerity is not really beautiful, and frankness without beauty does not reveal the truth in all sincerity.

All disputes and disagreements, all misunderstandings fall away, the moment that one's spirit has become noble. It is the sign of the noble spirit to comprehend all things, to assimilate all things, to tolerate and to forgive. What use is religion, philosophy or mysticism if these do not awaken in one that very spirit which is divine?

A flower proves to be genuine by its fragrance, a jewel proves to be genuine by its radiance, a fruit proves to be genuine by its sweetness, and a person proves to be genuine by the beauty and sincerity of the personality.

Softening of the Ego

When Jesus Christ said, "Blessed are the poor in spirit," that message revealed the true secret of the 'Art of Personality,' understood in that context as being the effacement of one's own ego. Since one knows for oneself that, in life, it is the ego of others which disturbs one the most—therefore, as a service to others, one chooses willingly to efface one's own ego.

The words, "poor in spirit," clearly illustrate the softening of the ego, which then has a certain charm. This same charm is also seen in persons who have experienced suffering and disappointment. Nevertheless, the true virtue in the softening of the ego lies in one's own initiative taken on the path of self-denial.

It is the gratification of the ego which builds up its strength, and the more satisfaction acquired, the greater is the desire. In so doing, one becomes enslaved by one's own ego, although being of divine origin. Really speaking, one should have the liberty of being king or queen in one's own domain, but through gratifying the ego, not only does one awaken the fighting spirit of others (whose egos are thereby disturbed), but one falls from sovereignty to slavery, becoming finally a burden even to oneself.

The great battle which the wise fight is a battle with the self, whereas an unthoughtful person fights with the ego of others. In these battles, the victory of the unthoughtful is a temporary one, but the victory of the wise is permanent. However, when battling with one's own ego, it is very difficult to know with whom one is really fighting, because one only sees the limited aspects of the self which together form the illusion of one's own individuality. Yet, when digging deep within the limitations of the self, one might perhaps discover the truth of the real self. It is then that the annihilation of the 'false self' becomes a clear answer to the inner call.

The finer the ego, the less disturbing it is to others, but life's trials become that much harder to endure. A thorn does not harm its likeness, but it can destroy the frailty of a delicate rose. Nevertheless, life is profoundly lived as a rose, with its beauty, colour and fragrance, rather than living as a thorn among thorns.

The Training of the Ego

The training of the ego does not necessarily require a life of renunciation. It is, rather, a test of balance and of wisdom. Such a training implies the understanding of the reason behind a desire, of what might be the consequences of obtaining satisfaction, of whether or not one can afford the necessary price, and of whether it is a righteous or an unjust desire.

Under the spell of a desire, one's senses of justice, logic and duty are muted by the grip of the ego. In that state of mind, one judges according to one's perceived best interests, one reasons from the point of view of selfishness, and one's feelings of duty are darkened by one's all-pervading image of self.

No doubt it is difficult to discriminate between right and wrong, between that which is natural and that which is not, between that which is really necessary and that which is not, and between that which brings happiness and that which leaves sorrow. Here again, the answer is found in the training of the ego, by which one comes to realize that one's worst enemy as well as one's best friend, which is wisdom, are both within oneself.

Self-consciousness

Self-consciousness has endless facets, some reflecting inferiority complexes, such as the need for praise and admiration, and others arising from superiority complexes, such as satisfaction in humiliating and dominating others, with an unquenchable thirst for self-assertion. The more one tries to dissimulate one's weakness behind a mask of outer appearance, the more one's self-confidence collapses like a sand castle under the waves of the rising sea. However, when the ego is softened, it harmonizes in all circumstances, like the little bubbles which float along with the waves even in a stormy ocean.

Life could be pictured as a building with doors smaller than one's own size. At every attempt to go through, one knocks one's head against the door-frame, leaving no other device than bending the head when passing through the door.

Modesty is not necessarily weakness, nor is it the same as humility, if that is founded upon self-pity. Modesty is a feeling which rises from the living heart which is secretly conscious of its inner beauty, while at the same time veiling itself even from its own sight.

The Meaning of Dharma

The Hindu word for religion is *dharma*, which means 'duty.' It could also be understood as consciousness of one's most noble obligations. When attuned to the deep meaning of this interpretation of religion, one realizes that to be religious means to accomplish those duties which have been entrusted to us by destiny as the purpose of our lives.

Therefore, as workers in the cause of love, harmony and beauty, it is our most religious duty to practise the 'Art of Personality,' so that we might some day become living examples of those ideals, while dancing the sacred dance at the 'Court of Indra', the temple of the 'Divine Presence' found within our hearts.

VI. Everyday Life
Taqwa Taharat

The Nature of the Mind

The nature of the mind is to hold an impression, which is called 'memory'. As a consequence, a thought is held in the mind, whether it is beneficial or not, without consideration of what might be the outcome of this retention. Many retain a thought of pain or unkindness, without realizing the consequences of discomfort and distress for themselves and for others. This can be compared to a child holding a rattle and hitting its own head with it, yet not throwing it away, although the blow was painful.

Will Power

Concentration is practised for the purpose of gradually developing will power, which helps in making a better use of one's faculties. One tries to remember the impressions which are worth remembering, and to wipe out those which it is preferable to forget, freeing oneself thereby from that which disturbs one's peace of mind.

Will power not only helps to hold a thought in mind, but it also helps to keep away all unwanted thoughts, strengthening thereby the ability to free the memory from those disturbing impressions which cover it like the darkening shadows of clouds. Failure has no grip upon a progressive person who is able to retain in mind the thought of success, however many failures might come along, knowing that a standstill is the greatest handicap to all further progress.

To the question, "Which among the impressions received should be preserved and which of them should be eliminated in the pursuit of happiness and success?" the answer is, preserve all those that are beautiful, harmonious and peaceful, and eliminate all those which are void of such qualities, because the mind cannot function successfully when it is hindered by negative impressions that disturb its inner peace.

Releasing Unwanted Impressions

Among unwanted impressions, some have to be buried under the earth; others drowned under the waters so that they never come to the surface again; still others must be burnt to ashes, like wood in the fire; while some can just be shaken away like dust in the wind; and still others are simply erased from the very surface of the mind in an absolute annihilation, as though they had never ever been there.

Anything that weighs upon the mind, such as worry, fear, remorse or guilt, keeps the mind attuned to a pitch which is below its natural tone. When in that state of mind, even the most capable person cannot function efficiently, being thereby unable to accomplish those ideals for which he or she is striving.

The Master-mind

Since all things in life are accomplished by the power of the mind, which works as an engineer, it is therefore essential that the mind should be in full control of all parts of the machinery. Just as one pebble can cause disorder in an entire mechanism, so one undesirable thought can be the cause of lack of success in one's life. One often feels helpless when confronted with difficult conditions, but one seldom realizes that the problem lies within oneself alone. It is like standing in front of a barrier, not seeing that one has a hammer in one's hands with which any obstacle could be overcome. That great tool is our will power. The mind, our will power, is all power that there is, if only one could realize the importance of becoming a master-mind over oneself.

Ethics

Naturally, questions arise concerning such concepts as good and bad, right and wrong, and other moral standards, which are not always understood in the same way by the followers of different religions, different cultures and different ethnic customs. Perhaps one could say that wrong-doing causes discomfort to the mind from the effects of an unrestful conscience, whereas righteousness brings comfort to the mind. However, one might ask, "How good, really, was the righteous one if, after doing good all one's life, one still had not found happiness?" The answer is that, if standards regulating right and wrong are made to fit artificially with customs and creeds, there can never be true justice. Each must learn to consult one's own spirit and to make a distinction between right and wrong from one's own feelings.

The Secret of Harmony

Harmony is brought about by attuning oneself to all beings and all circumstances. When one is not able to tune oneself to situations, but tries instead to tune others, it is then that the string breaks, so to speak, for each one has his or her own note, and it is as if one were tuning the string of a cello to the pitch of a violin.

By nature, all souls are in search of harmony, but few really know the secret of harmonizing with disharmony, which then disappears like a shadow in the rays of the sun. In music, every note is fitted to a definite pitch. In the same way, each person has his or her own fixed ideas and habits. Yet the one who is in search of harmony is attuned to all the notes, and could therefore be seen as the key tone which is at the basis of a consonant chord, wherein all notes sound harmoniously together.

The Fountain of Happiness

Real will power is proven when fighting with oneself, keeping away all undesirable impressions and impulses, thereby radiating harmony and peace, bringing happiness to oneself and to others.

Earthly pleasures are but the shadows of happiness because of their transitory nature. True happiness is in love, which is a stream springing forth from the heart. When this secret spring has been discovered, there is a constant outpouring of this stream of love and one becomes like a divine fountain. Then the mind is constantly purified from all which is inharmonious and which causes unhappiness.

Life on earth is not meant to be lived in unhappiness, even though lived righteously. Happiness cannot be replaced by righteousness, but righteousness springs forth from happiness. No soul is really deprived of even a glimpse of happiness, because the very nature of the soul itself is happiness. There are only clouds of unhappiness which fall as shadows upon the mirror of the soul, the mind. Once that mirror is cleared of all darkness, new power springs forth, opening surprising ways and means for the accomplishment of one's ideals. Then all obstacles are removed, leaving only place for success, which is attracted to one in abundance.

The Natural Self

It is very necessary in the life of an adept on the spiritual path to adapt body, mind and heart appropriately. Concentration, meditation and other practices all help the spirit to rediscover its natural condition, its original self. However great the musician, if the musical instrument is not in tune, not in its natural condition, the player is unable to express the beauty of the music as he or she would wish. Therefore, to become spiritual means to purify the spirit so that it discovers its natural self, which then may be expressed within the vehicles of body, mind and heart. Inasmuch as these reflect divine light, they become together the sacred 'Temple of God'.

VII. Metaphysics
Tasawwuf

Belief

Belief is a natural tendency, which continues in its chosen course like a stream of water flowing peacefully onwards until it strikes a rock standing in the way. The rock could be understood to be the stubborn resistance of reason, which claims the support of facts, and the stream of belief must sooner or later come in conflict with it. However, the believer is thereby enlightened by the bright light of intelligence coming from within, and when belief and reason have overcome their conflict, one speaks no more of belief, but of conviction. However, belief can also be unmoving, like frozen water, in which case there is a lack of progress.

Truth

Truth knows no boundaries, as long as one's belief is built upon conviction and guided by the light within, which leads one through all experiences—physical, mental as well as those of the feeling heart, onto the final path. Naturally, since we are all different, one belief cannot possibly be the right belief for all. When adopting another person's belief, out of consideration, one could very well be giving oneself away to something that one might regret. On the other hand, if another person's belief offers an opportunity of enrichment and one closes the door of one's heart, one shall sooner or later regret not having had more insight at the moment.

Faith

Faith, which is born in the heart, is like a bridge that links heaven and earth. It is a great power which can draw aside numerous covers of doubt and fear, leading ultimately to the accomplishment of one's ideals, whether here or in the hereafter. However, hope alone, without faith, can be limited in its perseverance, when one's patience runs out of steam. The symbol of patience is the cross, in which the vertical line indicates activity and the horizontal line, the power of mastery. Patience can doubtless be seen as crucifixion, whereas mastery, when it is the result of self-abnegation, is resurrection.

The Conscience

The human being has been granted, by nature, the ability to rise above the limitations of the false self (or ego) through the discovery of the inner torch, which annihilates the darkness of pride and ignorance. In the light of this torch, one can distinguish between right and wrong according to one's own understanding of justice, as well as evaluate the proportion of reality and illusion in all levels of consciousness.

When the inner light of the conscience is darkened, the sense of justice is distorted by egotistical interests, which overpower all logical considerations. It is also distorted when the sense of discrimination slumbers under the effect of temptation, in which case one's ability to discern between right and wrong is enslaved. Furthermore, in the absence of that same inner light, a clash of opinions occurs when different levels of knowledge see the same subject from different angles.

The conscience is, in itself, an entire world of its own and, as such, it is as real as the outer world. The finer the person, the finer the conscience. One person may, perhaps, repent more intensely than another for the same wrong-doing. No doubt what is right for one can be wrong for another, but in each and every case, it is the conscience which tests what is right or wrong and which voices the result. A good action brings happiness, whereas that which deprives one of tranquillity of mind, cannot be right.

The Higher Call

The conscience, which rises and falls like waves in the ocean of the mind, can yet be overwhelmed by the tide of love, which answers to a higher call, while the boat of action floats on towards its purpose. Like water underground, love is hidden, either close to the surface or deep down underneath. It is love which motivates the power of the mind and, with the help of which, thought becomes clear and fertile. Like the plant which springs forth from the earth, nourished by falling rain, so does love spring forth from within the heart, revealing its divine nature.

Spirituality

Religion, prayer and meditation are all seen as methods by which love, which is a divine heritage, is brought to the surface. In fact, it is love which is itself happiness, and the lack of love which constitutes unhappiness, like a compass needle which must point to the opposite pole when the polarity is reversed.

Various interpretations are given to the concept of spirituality. It is seen as being holy, melancholy, wonder-working or as some strange religiousness. However, what should be understood by spirituality, is none other than the realization of the soul discovering its own evidence, when rising and experiencing the Divine, and then falling back again within itself, which is also divine.The saintly person, for whom religion consists of seeking the pleasure of God, is most caring for the feelings of others, knowing that causing harm displeases God. The attunement of the heart to the will of God develops through awakening the sense of harmony, which the lover of beauty experiences on the path of self-effacement to the Divine.

*The attunement of the heart
to the will of*

God

*develops through
awakening the sense of*

Harmony

*which the lover of beauty
experiences on the path
of self-effacement
to the Divine.*

Githas

I. Attainment

II. Psychology

III. Mysticism

IV. Health

V. Uruj and Nazul

VI. Polarity in Breath

VII. Esotericism

VIII. Concentration

IX. Meditation

X. Spirit Phenomena

I. Attainment

The Goal of Life

There is no one in the world who is not striving for something or other. For some the purpose of life is clear, and for others it is perplexing. Whatever the goal, though, whether it be a material or a spiritual one, if one has not discovered the kingdom of God within one's heart, one has not yet realized what is one's true purpose in life.

The light which shines out from the very depth of one's being is equally as important as the goal for which one is striving. Therefore, one must never let the rope loosen in one's hands, even when faced with disillusionment or when crushed by the burden of doubts regarding one's own abilities. Such doubts often arise from the jealousy one might feel when comparing one's fate to the luck of others, who seem to be more fortunate at that moment. However, a loss can prove to be a gain in the end, and a gain can prove to be a loss.

Renunciation

Happiness is a birthright, yet wisdom inspires renunciation of projects which are either contrary to one's conscience or obtained at the cost of the suffering of others. Besides, among those values which are inconsiderately passed on from one to another without taking into account the law of cause and effect, those values which are preferable are certainly the everlasting ones.

Renunciation does not mean killing the desire, but rather realizing its true purpose. Indeed, renunciation out of doubt and fear, only kills the spirit. Desire itself is smaller or less important then the object of longing, but when obtained, both object and desire seem equally small. If one clings to the object of one's desire once it has been attained, one falls beneath one's own true values. However, if one renounces the illusion of both desire and object, one rises above their boundaries.

Success

In a successful action, the will power holds the reins of reason. If it is the other way around, there will be obstruction. If will power and reason are attuned to each other in mutual understanding, there will certainly be success in view. However small an object may be, when once it is taken up it must be accomplished, not necessarily for the benefit of the object itself, but what is more important, for the experience of perseverance. For each accomplishment is a step toward another goal, and as high is the goal, so high does one rise.

When fascinated by a project that one wishes to accomplish, several questions should be taken into account, such as, "Do I earnestly wish to accomplish this? Am I really aware of the sacrifice, the time and energy involved? Is the environment appropriate? Shall I prove to be worthy of the success which may perhaps come my way?" After such considerations, be obstinate and determined on the path of success, and only renounce when the goal is reached. True satisfaction is only experienced when rising above one's accomplishment, knowing that if the price paid was greater than the true value of the object, nevertheless, the difference will be credited in the form of greater experience when setting out on the next journey on the path of attainment, either material or spiritual.

Grace

There is a belief in all religious traditions, according to which unseen help is granted when invoking the grace of great saints and masters whose image symbolizes prosperity and spiritual guidance. It is undeniable that when love and devotion are kindled, one's heart becomes a receptacle of all positive influences coming in reply to one's yearning. This love and devotion is the truest secret of all the power required for the accomplishment of an ideal.

II. Psychology

Powers of Action and Thought

Just as there are rails on which a train travels, in the same way, tracks are traced in our lives, along which the wheels of our actions roll either smoothly or chaotically, according to our will power. While travelling along the track of life, one gradually discovers that there are two basic guiding rails in our lives, the unknown *karma* (or destiny) and the known *dharma* (or duty). During the journey, it could occur that the wheels might slip off the rails, owing to a lack of self-discipline, and the consequence could be detrimental both to ourselves and to others.

The power of thought is greater than that of either word or action, but when all these three are harmonized, the power is far greater still. Then the breath runs like a golden thread through each as a spark kindling the thought, as an impulse creating the word, and as the energy of action. This explains why purity of breath is so important. While transiting the level of thought, the breath leaves traces of those vibrations experienced in both directions: action expressing thought, or thought commanding action. The vibrations perceived produce direct effects on one's state of mind, and condition the atmosphere of one's surroundings.

Auto-suggestion

Imagination can play a surprising role in our lives, especially when strengthened by superstition. Under the spell of superstition, one becomes the slave of one's own weakness of character, and adopts a pessimistic attitude, which is like the end of a path leading nowhere. Often, when unaware of the power of the mind-world, one's thoughts become entangled in a spider's web of auto-suggestions. Through negative thinking one either induces others into the labyrinth of one own ideas, or one is unconsciously an impediment to one's own expectations.

Auto-suggestion can attract or repel whatever situation one wishes to create for oneself or for others. In this way, it is the secret of happiness and success. Nevertheless, a gain in one thing can be the cause of a loss in another thing and, reversibly, a loss in one thing can be the cause of a gain in another thing.

Every atom has a particular force of attraction and, under the spell of wealth, power and position, one does not always foresee the consequences of this charm, if one's psychic power acts without a ray of wisdom to clarify the darkness of self-assertion. When wisdom leads and the psychic power guides, however, both together have the power to rule over destiny.

The Power of the Motive

In the constant struggle of gain and loss, gain is always on the side of the one who holds courageously to the motive, for providence supplies support unconditionally to one's perseverance, without discrimination as to the moral values of the motive. Therefore, it is precisely at this point that the responsibility of each person is put to the test, as far as the beneficial or destructive aspect of the motive is concerned.

Psychic power is developed through making use of thought, which becomes creative when a motive is in view. Yet, paradoxically, as soon as a thought is formed, it is thrown off by the restless movement of the mind, which is in a continual state of unfoldment and can only hold a thought in place with the help of will power. When the mind is under control, however, a thought can be focused with the power of an arrow, carrying with it all good or bad feeling. This is why it is so important to be constantly aware of the cause and effect of all one's thoughts—not only the conscious ones, but also the unconscious ones. Like plants, motives have their roots in the mind, and are watered by will power. Therefore, undesirable thoughts must be avoided with all care.

Psychic power is like a spring of running water, whereas the motive creates a channel along which the stream of water flows. As many motives as there are, so many channels will there be. So many times the power of the motive is divided, leaving less and less scope for successful accomplishment. Therefore, the power of accomplishment is very much dependent on the priority allotted to the motive.

Nevertheless, if the feeling heart is the inspirer of the motive, all power required is constantly present and, through the fire of love, the motive becomes, at last, an ideal.

III. Mysticism

The Nature of Manifestation

All life is one and the same abstract consciousness (*Brahma*), which manifests in as many rays as there are beings. Manifestation is, so to speak, the crystallization of abstract consciousness within a framework or *akasha*, wherein it is all-pervading, just as it is in all space.

Within this framework or material body, abstract consciousness becomes intelligible to the seer as different vibrations producing light of various colours, corresponding to the influences of the five elements, which contain the secret code of creation on our planet Earth.

Out of the innumerable energies which are distinguishable in the human being, one which is neither visible nor tangible is breath, or *prana*. It is along the flow of the incoming and outgoing breath that the different rhythms inherent in the five elements are channelled to and from the mind world in waves of impulses via the five senses.

This explains why colours are seen at different times of day and night by those whose breath is pure and subtle, and who have acquired the technique of directing the flow of breath in various directions, corresponding to the natural tendencies of the elements: spreading, flowing, rising, penetrating, and elevating.

Movement is induced by the law of attraction. Opposite forces, the creative or *jelal* and the receptive or *jemal*, seek to complete each other within the capacity of a third force, *kemal*, which is neutral, being at the same time the source of all energy and the culmination of *jelal* and *jemal*, wherein their natures lose all creative and receptive characteristics.

When the breath happens to be under the spell of the creative energy, *jelal*, there is a natural tendency to act positively, to take decisions, to start projects and defend one's rights. Under the spell of the receptive energy, *jemal*, one is resigned, communicative, well-disposed and open to inspiration. The *kemal* energy, which is life itself and creative of all energies, is beyond distinctions and differences. When attuned to this energy, one finds oneself face to face with the divine will, and all material interests lose their hold because both the creative and the receptive dispositions are sublimated therein.

IV. Health

Balance and Rhythm

Health depends upon a certain balance in the activities of the five senses, which are expected to respond to incoming impressions while being under control of the mind. In this respect, the wise attach a certain importance to developing the art of directing the activities of the senses and, in so doing, balancing the proportion of activity and repose so as to avoid useless loss of energy. Nevertheless, it must be understood that a general rule cannot be made because a certain amount of activity is also stimulating, in different proportions in each case.

The senses can be kept in balance through the proper application of various simple activities such as sitting, lying, standing and walking, as well as through regularity in eating, drinking, working, resting and sleeping. Really speaking, most troubles are caused by an inappropriate rhythm, as when the clock ticks either too fast or too slow, and then all goes out of order. Rhythm is the source from which magnetism springs, just as electric energy is born from the steady rotation of a dynamo. It is the lack of magnetism which causes discomfort and pain, whereas the development of magnetism secures physical and mental well-being.

Since breath is life itself and the five senses are coordinated through the power of breath, it is clear that by developing the breath's volume and its length, so that it becomes both intense and extensive, and by emphasizing its structured rhythm, one is deepening the consciousness behind the five senses. In this respect, one may speak of three characteristic types of breath. In one, there is no distinguishable rhythmic count, either in the inhalation or the exhalation, and the breath becomes thereby chaotic at times. In the second type of breath, the inhalation and exhalation have different counts, each being based on a different rhythm. In the third type of breath, the inhalation and exhalation are perfectly equal, and they can eventually be made to correspond to the beats of a *wazifa* or sacred word or phrase.

Spiritual Healing

This combination of breath and thought, repeated a number of times, is used to a great extent in spiritual healing. If one knows how to direct breath, one is able to intensify the light current and to send it to any part of the body, communicating strength to overcome pain, weakness and congestion.

Human beings are more conscious of the material world than of any other, and for this reason, possessing or even just holding magnetized objects or charms has brought about great healing. This takes place because the one from whom those objects were received had magnetized them with the healing power of breath and, therefore, the presence of the healer is always felt. Of course, it is imperative that the healer should communicate piety, spirituality and kindness, and so the healer attaches great importance to purity of mind at every level.

In spiritual healing, it is the work of the mind which is the greatest. Therefore, the power of concentration is the first thing to develop. It should be developed to such an extent that the designated object of concentration is not only visualized mentally, but also even with the eyes open during normal daily life. The power of concentration should be such that the spiritual healer is able to visualize the patient in a perfect state of health.

A warm-hearted spiritual healer creates a charged atmosphere which is just as important as concentration. Nevertheless, prayer is an essential source of healing magnetism, for without the thought of God, all concentration is held powerless within the limitations of one's own personality. Prayer in thought is certainly the most subtle means of attunement to the 'Divine Presence,' but when prayer is put into words, it becomes even more concrete and more effective for healing purposes.

In this connection, it is important to know that, through the practice of *Zikar*, a spiritual healer develops the power of voice which then reaches to the depth of the heart of the patient. The eyes also offer a powerful means of healing through the radiance of sight, which is soothing to pain and sorrow.

The Hands and Absent Healing

The Hindus have pictured the personification of the Divine with four hands, of which two symbolize the hands of the mind. It is true that if the hands are well synchronized, the healing activity is perfectly accomplished. Therefore, in spiritual healing, the hands of the healer also represent the hands of the mind, because the power of the mind can be channelled through the hands.

Every atom in the body is radiant and this explains why spiritual healing can be effective when practised even with the finger tips, in the same way a musician can reproduce deep feelings with the touch of the fingers on the piano keys. It is not simply the placing of the fingers on the keys which produces the beauty of the tone, it is the song of the feeling heart which is thereby communicated. In the same way, it is the loving compassion of the spiritual healer, directed to the finger tips, which brings about spiritual healing.

Moses is known to have held light in the palms of his hands (*Yadi Baiza*), and Zoroaster is often pictured with burning fire in his hands. These and many more examples suggest the radiance which can be awakened in the human hands. When that radiance is developed, it shines out through the finger tips and can be directed to any chosen area. Magnetism running through the finger tips, penetrates into everything that a spiritual healer holds in his or her hands. This explains why magnetized water, which the Persians call *abi hayat* or water of life, can also have healing power, water being receptive to vibrations or *prana*.

In absent healing, or healing at a distance, the mastery of *Fikar* helps to hold in thought, the image of the patient in a perfect state of health. Distance makes no difference when the power of the breath of the healer is attuned to the breath wavelength of the patient. It is belief that gives the power to heal, revealing thereby that thought knows no distance. However, the strength of that belief is revealed only when "I am" is replaced by "Thou art." Whatever be the gifts of the spiritual healer, if there is a lack of self-confidence and faith, all theories become powerless.

In Hindu metaphysics, *Nada Brahma* or 'Sound-God', is referred to as being life's secret. This is so because sound is motion, and nothing takes place without energy of some type as the source of motion. When attuned to *Nada Brahma*, and when all disciplines that have been acquired are harmoniously coordinated, the healing power will find its way through the heart of the one who truthfully becomes a humble channel with the purpose of receiving and transmitting the divine healing power, as a service to God and humanity.

V. Uruj and Nazul

Phases of the Breath

Breath, which is life itself, may be understood to have two phases, known by Sufis as *uruj* and *nazul*. In *uruj* or inhalation, the breath draws within us the conditions of our surroundings. During *nazul* or exhalation, the breath projects outward our own inner condition. The harmonious or inharmonious state of our exhaled breath, first affects the mind, then the physical condition, and finally, even our surroundings. Similarly, the harmonious or inharmonious conditions of our surroundings are first drawn into our body, then penetrate to the mind, and finally affect even the condition of our innermost being.

The rise and fall of *uruj* and *nazul* are the very basis of one's entire being. Spring and Autumn, day and night, sunrise and sunset, and the waxing and waning of the moon, all reveal the same principle—there is no rise without a fall, and no fall without a rise. Since we represent the world in miniature, all of nature's characteristics may be found within. Additionally, as breath is life itself, the rhythmic rise and fall of our breath has great influence upon our physical and mental condition and, consequently, also upon our behaviour in daily activities, which may be thereby rendered either harmonious or chaotic.

Although there is a hidden purpose in both the rise and fall of nature, yet in appearance, a rising prospect is preferable to a falling one. Therefore, the master-mind regulates the rhythm of the rising principle, thereby making sure that the timing of the natural falling aspect is kept within control.

Breath and Action

Life, as we understand it, is the consciousness of existence and existence is perceived in all activities. We also know that activity, whether physical or mental, is fully dependent upon the power of breath. This power is generated by the energy of the alternating polarity *uruj* and *nazul*, the rhythm of which conditions our physical and mental abilities. The nature and rhythm of the breath can adopt one of the three characteristics known by Sufis as *jelal, jemal* or *kemal*. When breath is flowing through the right nostril, the *jelal* polarity is active. When breath is flowing through the left nostril, the *jemal* polarity is active. The *kemal* condition results from a fusion between the two polarities, with a chaotic effect on material activities, but an uplifting attraction in activities involving spiritual attunement.

Knowing this, it becomes obvious that activities which would be successful during the rising power of *uruj* would not be advisable during *nazul*, and vice versa. Just as the sun rises, reaches the zenith and sets, in the same manner the light of the mind shines brilliantly while *uruj* (the energy of action) prevails, overwhelming all reason and logic. That same light arrives at the zenith when a project reaches its culmination, a *kemal* condition. Thereafter comes a second phase, in which the initial enthusiasm starts to decline, referred to as *nazul*. This is followed by a third phase, which the Sufis call *zaval*, when the light of the mind is no longer focused upon the project, but rests in a state of inertia, overwhelmed by the fall of action following the project's accomplishment.

VI. Polarity in Breath

The Five Elements

All elements are present, to a greater or lesser degree, in all of nature's creation. Similarly, in each element, all the colours of the rainbow may be seen, although one specific colour is predominant. In addition, the elements represent different characteristics. For instance, 'earth' has the tendency to spread, 'water' to flow onward, and 'fire' to rise. 'Air' may be said to possess all tendencies and 'ether' is above definition. All these tendencies are recognizable in one's breath, along which the elements flow, by turn, all through the day and night. This explains why persons of different temperament may harmonize at certain times and not at others.

It is the fire element which makes one person rise in anger against another, while the water element in one's nature has a subduing effect. The earth element is responsible for our preconceived ideas, and the air element is a handicap when making decisions.

Power of Breath

The power of breath is also related to other major factors such as the opposite polarities of *jelal* and *jemal*. The *jelal* nature is courageous, determined and expressive, whereas the *jemal* nature is receptive, kind and inspiring. These two polarities, called *Shiva* and *Shakti* in Vedantic terms, may be likened to the sun and moon. The *kemal* condition is the simultaneous activity of both polarities, resulting in the annihilation of the very nature of each, and creating a perfect balance. Paradoxically, this produces failure in material activities, but is a source of spiritual attunement where the annihilation of the self prevails, called in poetic terms, 'The Bowl of Poison of Mahadeva.'

It is clear that, besides physical and mental efforts, there are great powers available which may help one to accomplish one's ideal. However, any abuse or misuse of these powers, such as thought-reading or prophesying for egoistical purposes, contradicts the noble principles of mysticism, and can never be of any real profit nor prove to be of any spiritual value.

VII. Esotericism

Prayer

Contemplation of divine grace builds up a God-ideal in the mind, which in turn awakens love in the heart. When love streams forth from the heart in rays of light, the illusion of darkness is dispelled and the horizon of the devotee is enlarged, so that all things become clear and the false aspects of one's being surrender to the 'All-pervading,' the 'Only Being.' This contemplation, the first and last practice on the spiritual path, is called *nimaz*, or prayer.

Breath Purification

When breathing upon 'earth,' the breath is purified by the vibrations of that steady element, which offer a feeling of strength and stability, both mental and physical.

When breathing upon 'water,' the breath is purified by the vibrations of that moving element, which offer movement in all activities and even reactivation or redirection of a stagnant situation.

When breathing upon 'fire,' the breath is purified by the vibrations of that powerful element, which offer energy and excitement in all circumstances.

When breathing upon 'air,' the breath is purified by the vibrations of that uplifting element, which offer inspiration and peace.

When breathing in the awareness of 'ether,' the breath is purified by the vibrations of that spiritual element, which offer unfoldment and light.

Wazifa

Words are the echo of thoughts, and thoughts are the echo of emotions, which finally find expression when the words are spoken. Conversely, words, which become images in the mind, can at last penetrate to the feeling heart. *Wazifa*, called also Mantra Yoga in the Vedanta, means the repetition of a sacred word, the influence of which is most beneficial, physically and psychologically. For spiritual enlightenment, the sacred names of God, symbolizing idealized attributes, are used. As many times as a *wazifa* is repeated, that many times it is recorded within the heart. Nevertheless, purity of purpose and regularity of rhythm, time and circumstances are also most important.

Zikar

Zikar, also called Mantra Yoga by the Vedanta, is a *Kalma Kalman*, meaning a meditative, rhythmic repetition of the sacred name of God. The Sufis of all ages have expressed this with the words, "*La el la ha, el Allah hu,*" meaning "God alone exists," repeated either in a spoken or chanted meditation while gently rotating the torso in perfectly synchronized movement.

When chanting the melodic pattern which, as given by Pir-o-Murshid Inayat Khan, is structured according to the specific *Raga Bhairvi*, the entire being of the *zakir* is uplifted by the sacredness of the musical inspiration, called *Ghiza-i-Ruh* or 'food of the soul,' as well as being attuned to the magic swing of the rhythmic beats.

During *Zikar*, the body of the *zakir*, intensely tuned to the rhythm, becomes itself the repeated word. The sacred phrase becomes like a glowing flame. The voice radiates great warmth and light, and the breath of the *zakir* becomes life itself. As Shams Tabriz said, "Say Allah, and Allah shalt thou become."

Fikar

Breath is life itself, and neither the body nor the mind can function without it. Therefore, with the breath, the very essence of life is absorbed, awakening thereby the individual consciousness, which becomes intelligible as coordinated thought is brought into motion.

The practice called *Fikar* is comparable to an elevator which raises one's consciousness from one level to another, starting within the denseness of the physical body, transiting the mind world, and finally reaching the ultimate heights, discovered within the feeling heart.

Just as rhythm is the nature of motion, so inhaling and exhaling are at the origin of all actions. When the breath is rhythmic, everything functions harmoniously. When the breath is chaotic, every initiative fails, the memory slumbers and the will power seems to have crept aside. *Fikar* is a combination of rhythmic breathing with the mental repetition of a *wazifa*. It can be done as a daily practice, either standing, sitting, lying or walking. The day comes when it continues, unconsciously, during one's daily occupations. It even goes on right into the night when one is asleep, becoming second nature, absolutely inseparable from one's normal breathing.

Kassab

Once one is awakened to the precious help which the *Fikar* practice offers in the way of securing a balanced condition in one's entire being, one then feels the need to relate that technique to one's thought and feeling as well. Herein lies the difference between *Fikar* and *Kassab*. Another difference is in the rhythm, because with *Kassab* there is a holding of the breath between the inhaling and the exhaling. For example, if the inhalation takes four beats and the exhalation takes four beats, the breath is held for eight beats.

Furthermore, while inhaling, one mentally absorbs the vibrations of a chosen *wazifa*. While holding the breath, one mentally assimilates those vibrations. While exhaling, one renders them to their source, with emotion and feelings of gratitude in one's heart. Besides this, the breath is either inhaled through the right nostril and exhaled through the left (a *jemal* breath), or conversely, inhaled through the left nostril and exhaled through the right (a *jelal* breath). In the third part of the practice, the exhalation is through both nostrils (a *kemal* breath) in order to create a balanced condition. The *Kassab* practice is derived from the Hindu *Pranayama* in Raja Yoga. However, there is a difference in the number of beats during the retention as well as in the direction of breath, and the addition of a held-out phase of the breath.

Shagal

In reality, there is no darkness. Life is light, omnipotent and omnipresent. When spreading or scattered, light appears to be dim or dark, but when centred it becomes bright. Therefore, the practice known as *Shagal* could be seen as the experience of drawing life forces to a centre, a centre of inner illumination.

This experience takes place without passing through the five senses, the idea being to reverse the sensory faculties so that they become conscious of the spirit within, which is the true 'seer.' In other words, when closing the senses to all incoming impressions, one finds oneself face to face with an open window upon the innermost depth of one's own being.

The *antarajnani*, or knower of the abstract world within, sees the light with closed eyes, hears the inner sound (called *anhad* or *sarmad*) with closed ears, and experiences all the other inner sensations while directing the breath inwardly, a practice called *Suram* or *Suara* or Swara Yoga.

The first stage in *Shagal* is called *Sulltani Nasurah*, and further steps are known as *Sultani Mahmud* and *Sultani Laskar*.

VIII. Concentration

Impressions

An impression is the shadow of events received through the five senses and traced unconsciously upon the screen of the mind. Similarly, will power is the light which illuminates the thought, enabling a coordination of colour and line in a creative and intelligible image.

Concentration fixes the impressions received and also helps to retain the thought. For this reason, memory is dependent upon correct observation, as it also is dependent upon will power for the creation of thought. In addition to the impressions received through the five senses, there are much finer ones which vibrate within the feeling heart. Just as a magnet holds metal by the power of attraction, in the same way, concentration can become very powerful when thoughts are steadily fixed in the mind by the magnetic power of the feeling heart.

Everything perceived through the five senses is stored deep down in the memory, but unless it is actively called upon, it is disorganized. When wanted, however, all the pieces are assembled, reconstructing the original image. In dreams, when the light of intelligence is on standby and the power of the will is slumbering, the regrouping of the thought-fragments lacks coordination, which explains the unreality of dream images. The same process during sleep is called dream, whereas in the waking state it is called imagination.

Concentration is the secret of all accomplishment in ourselves, in our affairs, and in our relationships with others. As simple as it is, this subject deserves to be an important study and practice in our lives. However, we only feel the importance to the extent that we understand it, although it stands as the basic mechanics of every yoga system since the beginning of time.

Will power plays the most important role in concentration. Its first action is to provide the impulse of thought which opens the storehouse of memory; secondly, to hold these various particles together, thereby creating the image upon which to concentrate. Those who accomplish great works and those who are successful in everything they undertake are possessors of strong will power. Will develops concentration, and concentration develops will.

Deconcentration

Concentration is meant to enable one to hold whatever impression one wishes, not only retaining it in the mind, but also building it up and projecting it any desired distance. Curiously enough, this same ability to concentrate can also help one to liberate oneself from undesirable impressions. This process, called deconcentration, requires even more will power than any other type of concentration.

Deconcentration, therefore, must be seen as a means of purifying the mind. As to observation, the more one can develop this ability, the more one shall discover the secret of strengthening the mind or, in other words, channelling the energy of will power, thereby developing the faculty of coordinated thinking. The consequence of all these efforts is an automatic development of the most precious of all mental faculties, the faculty of memory.

Inner Development

Accordingly, the first steps to be taken on the path of inner development are those of observation, concentration, creative concentration, projective concentration and deconcentration.

The power of an impression made upon the mind can be so great that it conditions one's perception at all levels—physical, mental, emotional and spiritual. In this way, the vibrations of an idealized image of worship may be reproduced upon the mirror of the soul.

The object of concentration inspires one to the extent that the heart is open to its message. However great the message might be, it still has no impact on the heart of the person whose feeling for devotion has not been awakened. The effect of a feeling heart can certainly be observed in the lives of great ones, whose deeds have been profoundly inspired by the admiration and devotion that they themselves have had for precious ideals, which were at the origin of all motivation.

Concentration has the power to bring about positive or negative results, either willingly or unwillingly, according to whether one is intentionally concentrating or passively viewing one's own mental obsessions. Therefore, it is clear that there is some danger in becoming a slave of the power of concentration, which happens when one is not able to delete unwanted thoughts.

For this reason, the two great powers of concentration, holding and erasing, should be developed simultaneously. The first is constructive, helping to bring about inner strength and steadiness of mind. However, the ability to delete thoughts helps to free the mind from worries and fears. This power could be called deconcentration.

Prayer

Prayer is a practice in concentration which can offer great upliftment. Yet, it can sometimes be a means of focusing one's thoughts upon oneself which is, of course, a hindrance to concentration, as well as being a heavy load pulling downwards all one's sincerest inner aspirations.

The most uplifting subject to concentrate upon is the personality of spiritual souls whom one has idealized and whose examples inspire either creative or spiritual guidance. Whatever be the chosen ideal, it is the intensity of one's devotion that will secure the beauty of the achievement.

However, when opening one's heart to God, finding oneself face to face with the 'Divine Presence,' at that very moment of self-redemption, one realizes that, what one thought was oneself, was only an illusion. Still, paradoxically, individual consciousness is at the same time God's consciousness, like the drop of sea water which is, at the same time, only just a drop, and yet, it is the sea itself in an individualized form. After concentration, this is the first and at the same time the ultimate lesson in meditation.

IX. Meditation

Consciousness Without Thought

Meditation is an escape from the outer world and a landing in the abode of the heart, where the consciousness is awake even in the absence of thought, where there are no limitations connected to physical or mental conditioning. One of the main purposes of meditation is to remove the thought, for a moment, from the mirror of individual consciousness, so that the mind may be illuminated by the light of the soul.

First, concentration upon a large circle places the mind under the power of the will. Then, when seeing the circle shrinking more and more, one experiences the separation of the thought from the self, until one is only focusing on the dot, which is at the centre of what is left of the circle. Now this dot, or spark of light, becomes a searchlight which guides the thought to higher levels of consciousness, where there is no difference between 'me' and 'Thee,' where the 'Divine Presence' is in the innermost depth of one's heart, where one meets with God, the omnipresent and all-pervading.

Cosmic Consciousness

When one awakens to higher consciousness, the temporary importance of all values fades away, for one is no longer possessed by them. Desire, for instance, which only leads to transient satisfaction, can cause one to confuse contentment with that happiness which is revealed in the absence of all notions of self-concern. When we roam toward the horizon of illusions, its countenance gently eludes us as we approach it, unless the journey to discover cosmic consciousness is free of all desire.

At this stage of true awakening, one is invariably enchanted by the great wonder-marks of creation, which trigger one's curiosity as to the whence and whither of a universe of light, sound, colour, form and energy. One feels the need to establish intelligible definitions, to define the undefinable. One makes many assumptions and attempts many improvisations to describe cosmic consciousness, and undoubtedly these reflect one's own state of mind as influenced by one's condition and circumstances.

Restraining the Mind

Mastery over the illusion of the self is obtained when restraining the mind from the uncontrolled recording of impressions. In doing so, rather than identifying oneself with the waves of thought awakened by the external stimulus of the senses, and modified by such influences as knowledge, discrimination and emotion, one offers repose to the thinking mechanism.

All thoughts and actions throw the mind world into corresponding waves. When a thought or action no longer occupies one's attention, one assumes that the thought waves have ceased, but there has only been a reduction in the intensity of their motion. That motion may stir again and again, throwing up stormy waters each time that one ventures to release the impression held in the storehouse of the memory. In other words, impressions, whether good or bad, could be seen as the denial of the ultimate pacification of the waters of the mind world.

The Seer from Within

The 'seer from within,' or *purusha*, is all intelligence. Yet, it is only through the 'ability to see,' or *prakriti*, the definition of the concept of individual consciousness, that the 'seer from within' sees.

The very nature of the 'seer from within,' the real self, is to experience its own reality, which is only a reality inasmuch as the 'ability to see' is there, this ability being at the same time the seer, the sight, and the purpose of seeing.

When drawing closer to spiritual awakening, one profoundly hopes to probe the depths of life, to discover the source and goal of all things, to unfold the mysteries of time and space, and of matter and spirit. In time, all earnest attempts on the path of the seeker finally contribute toward realizing the degree of one's own limitations. This realization awakens the feeling of humility, when once the doors of the heart are open, finding oneself face to face with the 'Divine Presence,' the living God within.

X. Spirit Phenomena

The Journey of the Soul

When referring to a soul which has passed on, the word 'spirit' is not an appropriate term because, really speaking, there is only one spirit, the spirit of all, from which all aspects of creation shine out as rays of life. The word 'spirit' is also misused in reference to botanical extracts, although the pure essence of a flower has fragrance only when it is dissolved in the air which we breathe, and through which it becomes perceptible.

The human spirit is of divine origin, shaped by influences experienced at the various stages of materialization through which it passes, on the way to becoming individual consciousness, as it is understood on the physical plane.

In reality, there is no such thing as a descent or an ascent of the spirit. If used at all, these terms merely illustrate the natural tendency of the soul, or individualized spirit, to feel attracted to physical experience. However, the real goal of the soul is to progress toward higher spheres, in a constant effort to rise above the limitations of the earth.

During the journey upwards, all experiences such as physical joys, pride of possession, feelings of friendship, responsibilities and attachments, are like chains which weigh the soul down. The further onward the soul journeys, the less it feels inclined to return to the body, which now seems like no more than a cast-off coat, and the personality, like a garment with which it was clad while on earth.

Obsession

It is common in all countries to tell ghost stories and fairy tales, which can be very exciting to the imagination and, in most cases, the exaggeration of facts indicates the belief in hidden manifestations. However, whether one believes or not, one cannot deny that there are cases where one can distinguish different personalities in one person, who may change in a moment, like lightning, from saintly to devilish.

A person with a passive mind, lacking initiative and feeling down-hearted, whose physical condition is weakened and whose will power is disturbed, is like an open window on the spirit world. It is mostly such a person who is subject to obsession, that is to say, to influences coming from departed souls who seek refuge in the receptive condition of others. A robust person, on the other hand, full of life and energy, in love with objects which are mostly materialistic, is like a stove where fire is choked by too much coal. In other words, the subtlety of the mind is clouded by too much self-consciousness and is therefore not receptive.

Influences and Apparitions

The presence of a soul which has passed on, is generally felt more than it is seen or heard. That presence brings either harmony or disharmony, according to the stage of evolution of the soul. Although one might think that one is free in thought and action, it is not always the case. Often one's thoughts and actions have been influenced in some way or other, perhaps just for a moment or in some cases for longer periods of time.

There are some cases of haunted houses where the influence of passed souls is strongly felt, but again, this same effect can be experienced in every home, inasmuch as the atmosphere of the present inhabitants also exerts a strong influence. In cases where an appearance has been experienced, this is only the image of a soul which manifests in one's mind, like a reflection seen in a mirror. In fact, it is the reproduction of life in the hereafter which manifests to the obsessed person, who may be either depressed or uplifted as a consequence. In other words, if the mind forms a concrete picture, that picture then appears to one in either a visible or audible form, which is called a phantom in spiritualist terms.

There are cases of obsession where the passed soul manifests with a certain purpose, either to offer guidance or to accomplish an unfinished task, and the obsessed person becomes an instrument at the mercy of the obsession. Therefore, spirit communication should not be taken lightly. It should be undertaken neither as a game nor an entertainment of any kind, especially for selfish or egotistic purposes.

Seen from another point of view, the power of annihilation is like the destiny of every drop splashed up by the ocean. If one cannot lose oneself in the thought of a loved one, one cannot lose oneself in God. The believer in God does not necessarily want to fulfill the ultimate purpose of belief. The next step is to lose oneself in the thought of a personality whom one idealizes, thereby bringing to life those qualities which one admires. The third step is an attunement with God, the one and only spirit, all spirit, spirit itself.

The motivation of the soul, when leaving this earthly existence, is to progress toward that destination which should be called fulfillment. There is not one single thought, word or action which does not reach its final destination, working through different spheres of manifestation in different guises, because every impulse that has once been set in motion goes on existing forever and ever.

The Only Secret

As we march courageously onward through the darkness of human ignorance, steadfastly displaying the banner of spiritual liberty, we may discover that the Sufi Message could be interpreted as an invitation to become living examples of love, harmony and beauty, to become living altars of all religious beliefs, to become a living confraternity of brothers and sisters.

As such, therefore, we should communicate the Message to each one in his or her own language, while safely guarding the only secret there is for inner peace, happiness and spirituality. What is that secret?

Each time we set aside our ego, even for a moment, we offer a little bit of our heart to the 'Divine Presence,' and in return, the light of the 'Spirit of Guidance' becomes brighter and brighter, until in the end, there remains no shadow to hide the perfection of the Only Being.

Sangathas

Extracts

Extracts

The divine ideal is found in the perfection of all things.

The origin of every impulse is divine, intelligible in different ways according to the degree of one's comprehension.

An impulse is a power in itself, and each time that the will creates an impulse it is drawing that energy from the cosmos, which in turn offers new strength to the will.

The world within is the reflection of the world without, but the inner life also has a great influence on the outer life.

The essence of life, manifested in nature, may be recognized in the flowers as perfume, in the elements as colour, in the rocks as precious stones—all of which are like blessings for the worshipper of God, who sees the divinity of manifestation in all creation.

Do not look for thanks or appreciation for all the good done to others, nor let your good deeds stimulate vanity—but do good for the sake of goodness, without even the thought of being recompensed.

The beautiful side in another person's nature is only seen if one is wishing to see it, but if one has no feeling of sympathy one only sees the shortcomings.

There are two main forces in life, one called *kaza* and the other called *kadr*. The one force is all-powerful and the other is merely one's own. This is experienced when, during the intoxication of an initiative, we force our way onwards until, suddenly, a much greater force blocks all attempts and we cannot proceed. This is what is meant by the words, "Man proposes and God disposes."

In every person there is one or more predominant elements which form the characteristics of that person's behaviour. The influence of the earth element is stability, the water cooperative, the fire enthusiastic, the air changeable, and the ether inspiring.

Nothing has an absolute value—it is the ideal, spiritual or material, which it represents that lends it worth.

As storm disturbs the ocean and the waves upset the surface, in the same way, earthly passions disturb the spirit, upset the mind, cause restlessness of the body, and result in useless turmoil.

The universe is an infinite mechanism and we are all parts of it. In spite of all our worldly knowledge or spiritual attunement, at times things do go wrong, because we are all part of the general scheme and cannot always expect the ocean to be without storms.

Everyone finds faults in others, but few recognize their own faults, and still fewer are those who make every possible effort to combat their faults.

The strength of thought, speech and action are related to the power of the feeling heart, and even so is the will the outcome of that same power within, upon which wisdom and success in life are completely dependant.

In all projects, first question oneself to be sure that there is no inner conflict. Only then shall one be convinced that success was already planned by providence. Thereafter, when taking the first step onwards, the second step shall surely be led by providence.

The soul is the offspring of the all-pervading spirit, and its goal is at the same time its source. Although temptations and attachments experienced during the journey detain it on its flight, it cannot ever feel fully satisfied till it reaches its destination.

Everything one sees could at the same time be audible, and all that is audible could at the same time be visible. In other words, the audible aspect might be hidden while the visible aspect is seen, and the visible aspect might be hidden while the audible aspect is heard. In the same way, when a pebble is thrown into a pool, one sees the horizontal circles growing larger and larger on the surface of the water, but one does not see the circles growing beneath the surface, as well as above, forming in reality perfect spheres, which go on unfolding in the infinite.

The theory of reincarnation is like a pill prescribed with the object of producing an immediate cure for those ill in spirit over the question of the justification of their deed and who try to bend the divine law so that it might fit in with man-made conceptions of right and wrong.

The reward or punishment for one's deeds is first felt within the heart before coming under the judgement of others, who see right and wrong from their own point of view, lacking insight into the cause behind the deed.

There are two aspects to all creation, the seen aspect and the unseen one. In Sufi terms these are called *zat* and *sifat*, also referred to in Vedantic terms as *purusha* and *prakriti*. The one is the known aspect of oneself with which we identify ourselves. The other is the unknown. The aspect which is always apparent keeps one limited within the boundaries of self-consciousness, whereas the unknown aspect, the spirit, is free of all limitations. It is by closing one's eyes to the known aspect of oneself that one discovers the reality of the hidden one.

When treading the spiritual path a battery is necessary, which is created by three principle morals: self-discipline, self-confidence and compassion. Like a plant, the spiritual power requires sunshine and water. The water is purity of life, and the sunshine is wisdom. Furthermore, a certain understanding of the value of retention is needed, so as to avoid useless waste of accumulated magnetism, which is built up all along the path of self-realization.

On the spiritual path, natural progress is advisable and, with conviction, one shall arrive safely at the soul's destination. If there is any visible sign of inner growth, it is seen in the softness of the feeling heart and in the humility of the attitude, which has nevertheless become that much more dignified and luminous, being thereby a living example for all.

Sangithas

Extracts

Extracts

The purpose of life, like the infinitely unfolding horizon which is never reached, appears to the seeker as an illusion, until having overcome the limitations of the concept of here and hereafter.

The heart is like an open window through which the light of the soul is projected upon the mind, and through which the impressions pictured in the mind are reflected back upon the soul.

In Hindu mythology, *Garuda* is the symbol of sound, suggesting that when riding on the flying bird, which is to say on the power of the sacred word which protects one from all that can harm, one does not hear that which one does not wish to hear; one does not see that which one does not wish to see; and one does not express that which one wishes to keep secret, for the inner experience of the sacred word can never be expressed.

There are some who express the desire to be corrected, but in reality it is an indirect appeal for praise, and if one misses the game by mentioning their faults, one only strengthens the roots of error in them. This creates disappointment on both sides, and one then regrets having lost an opportunity to withhold one's judgement. One cannot be of any help by emphasizing wrong-doings. It is through positive examples that the wrong can be improved. And in all cases, never allow a friend to become an enemy.

Self-assertion is sometimes found under the covers of humility and modesty which, like a mask, are used to hide pride, conceit, jealousy and envy—these being some of the many hindrances standing in the way of all spiritual progress.

True self-denial does not mean denying all things. It means denying the self to the self, this being the true attitude of the awakened heart. The heart is not made to belong simply to its limited self, and is only liberated to the extent that it resounds like a church bell to the striking upon its inner feelings. There comes a time, during the journey of self-realization, that every touch of beauty reminds one of the 'Divine Presence' and moves the heart to tears.

Real spirituality is living a life of fullness, with deep insight into all that comes ones way. Spirituality means raising ones consciousness from human to divine, by expanding the radius of the heart and by raising the consciousness experienced by the soul. Spirituality is, in itself, the forgetting of the self, while at the same time appreciating all, comprehending all, surmounting all and inspiring all.

The voice of the spheres is an accumulation of an infinitude of frequencies which together resound as one universal tone, audible in as many ways as it unfolds within each feeling heart. When the receptive channels of the five senses are inverted, the inaudible then resounds at an abstract level of consciousness.

Individuality is formed of all those characteristics which have been borrowed from various sources during the soul's journey to manifestation. How can one, therefore, ever say, "I am I," when nothing about 'me' is really 'me', except the illusion of being 'me'?

Wisdom inspires one to avoid forcing broad-minded ideas upon the small-minded, but rather to formulate one's thoughts in accordance with the level of understanding of each person.

It is best to offer all one's energy to any worldly activity in which one is expected to show responsibility and eagerness. Yet it is also wise to seek for divine consciousness whenever one can spare a moment to experience the great privilege of being recharged with inner strength and wisdom.

The one great moral to always follow, whatever be the circumstances in life, is to give without expecting anything in return, for in so doing one rises from slavery to sovereignty.

Spirituality is the unfoldment of inner nobility, the divine heritage of every soul, through which the origin of the soul is unveiled, and the more one is conscious of this, the more radiantly does it shine. Inner nobility is humility, modesty, kindness, graciousness—a manner which cannot be learned or taught, a manner which springs forth as a divine blossom. This is the highest religion, the truest spirituality. What use is religion, philosophy, morality or spirituality, if there is not an inclination to tolerate, to forgive, to comprehend, to harmonize, all of which are signs of divine manner? It is not by working wonders that one proves one's divine origin. If it is seen in anything, it is in the aristocracy of the soul and the democracy of the heart.

A flower attracts by its fragrance, a fruit by its sweetness, a jewel by its radiance, and a soul by its nobility of manner. A grass hut built on the foundation of truth is more lasting than a castle built on rocks.

Every individual is like a musical instrument which can be tuned to its own pitch. The instruments can also be assembled in an harmonious way so as to form an orchestra for which master-minds have composed music. This music is the true meaning of religion.

Let us never ignore the unstruck music

ringing constantly in our hearts.

May we venture to love

the charm of its

celestial melody,

so as to be in harmony

with the call

of Nature's Grace

in all beings,

becoming thereby

real and true

expressions of God's Beauty

Interpretations

The Individual as Seed of God

Here, Now and Hereafter

Light and Life

The Mystery of the Breath

The Individual as Seed of God
An Interpretation of the Githas

Out of the absolute, a consciousness was born—the consciousness of being conscious—and out of this consciousness arose the exaltation of existing. It is this exaltation which is understood by the ancient Greek word *logos*.

The oneness of the absolute, being concentrated upon a central point, then radiated as divine spirit, which may be conceivable as an opposite to darkness, although darkness is only a human illusion. Darkness could be understood as less light, and light as less darkness. These two opposing manifestations of consciousness then developed into an accommodation or *akasha*, a receptive capacity.

Every step taken by manifestation resulted in various shapes and substances, born out of the process of the involution of spirit, a path retraced at a later stage by the evolution of matter. In their structure, these various shapes and substances constitute different proportions of the four materialized elements—earth, water, fire and air, which are conceivable to us in accordance with the law of vibration, a law which becomes intelligible as we gain insight into the working of these elements. From these forms and substances the mineral, vegetable and animal kingdoms developed, followed by the human state—these developments providing, within the magnetic field of the ether element which is the source of all materialization of the divine, those *akashas* within which the rays of life found response.

In the human being, the purpose of manifestation is seemingly accomplished. Nevertheless, humanity has been entrusted with the responsibility of improving upon nature's creation and, in so doing, becoming more and more conscious of the divine origin from which all faculties have been inherited.

The understanding of the ether element has been esoterically elaborated upon by mystics in every age, and the various attributes of this element have been envisioned in the image of the sun, one of the first objects of adoration, and thereby the ancestral prototype of all religions. In other words, from ancient times symbols have been used to encapsulate the deepest subjects and most abstract concepts, for the limited understanding of humanity. Consequently, the sun was seen as the absolute, and the universal principle of contraction and expansion, seen in the sun's rising and setting, disclosed the secret of inhalation and exhalation, which is found as a fundamental law of all motion. This law of rhythm is interpreted by the mystics as 'the breath of God,' in which these two opposite motions are termed by the Sufis, *uruj* or expansion, and *nazul* or contraction. It is what could be understood intellectually by the term 'pulsation' which, seen from another point of view, is the secret of time.

The soul in its purest form, that is to say, a ray of divine light without any appreciation of self-consciousness, could be understood as an energy which has become individualized, roaming within a sphere which offers neither beginning nor end, neither past nor future, no condition and no object. In this condition, the soul is in a constant state of illumination, where the 'I' has no meaning, and all relative conceptions such as good and bad, happiness and sorrow, gain and loss and numberless other understandings, have no application. In this state, the soul is wandering freely in an enfoldment of everlasting light, which for human comprehension has been given the name angelic sphere.

The person whose heart is tuned to the pitch of the so-called angelic sphere will show, on earth, heavenly qualities. Spirituality could be understood as being the development of those very angelic qualities as reflections of love and light.

Intelligence, on the other hand, could be understood as being an inheritance of the qualities originating from another level, which could be called the sphere of mind or the *jinn* plane (from the Sanskrit word *jnana*, meaning the power of thought). The quality of this sphere is seen in the mind's hunger for knowledge. In this sphere of consciousness, where the soul becomes more captive then it was in the angelic plane, it is now perfectly conscious of the 'I' concept—wanting to be, and having forgotten that in the angelic planes it was without wanting to be. In this thinking condition, the soul is attracted by all those aspects of manifestation which tend to be definable, creating thereby imaginary dreams which do not yet have any relationship with logic or coordinated thought as it is experienced when the soul is embodied in the human image.

However, it is in the human form that that same thinking power, inspired by the heartfelt impressions from the angelic plane, experiences life on earth. Here the body is motivated by action, the mind is the consciousness which guides and accumulates experiences, and the heart is the clear mirror which reflects back upon the soul all that is experienced, without in any way modifying the brightness of the soul's light.

A child born on earth possesses thinking and feeling qualities which he or she may have inherited from parents and ancestors. At the same time, the child might also possess other qualities, some of which might be quite foreign to the parents, thus showing, right from the beginning of life, evidence of affinities to experiences to which he or she has never yet been exposed. For example, one finds among artists, poets, musicians, thinkers and creators of all types, traces of genius disposition which they might have absorbed as remnants of those impressions experienced in the sphere of pure intelligence, or *jinn* plane.

Obviously, just as one can be deeply impressed by events happening on the physical plane, the mind may also have been deeply impressed with the contact received in the *jinn* plane, and the feeling heart can very well be still resounding with the celestial vibrations of the angelic plane. For instance, souls that are inspired by the vibrations of the angelic plane, and souls impressed by the awakening of the *jinn* plane, all carry with them those deep impressions as they finally find themselves embodied in the physical being.

Similarly, on the return journey, the soul departing from the physical plane provides the *jinn* plane with its own world of memories and, when subsequently dissolving into the angelic plane, the undefinable vibrations of the feeling heart become one with the everlasting brilliance of that sphere. Thus the journey becomes a cycle, within which those arriving and those departing meet each other at the various levels of consciousness, that is to say, the level of action on the physical plane, the level of thinking on the *jinn* plane and at the level of spiritual exaltation on the angelic plane.

What opens the way for the soul to enter into a physical existence, if it is not the power of breath? Breath, which is the power behind all action, is that energy which keeps the entire mechanism in running order. It is the secret of birth and death. It is the current which flows through all planes of manifestation, and at the same time works as a coordinating power which assembles together action, thought and feeling in one individual being.

When the soul reaches the physical plane, it receives an offering from the universe. That offering is the body, which from then on is expected to function as a vehicle. This body is not only the product of the parents, but indirectly the product of the ancestors and the product of the entire human race. It is comparable to a lump of clay which has been kneaded thousands and thousands of times over, becoming more and more functional and more and more able to determine and coordinate actions. This lump of clay appeared first in the mineral kingdom, then developed in the vegetable kingdom, until it finally adopted the image that it has in each of us. In other words, the lump of clay has evolved from the most dense condition possible into a living being wherein, through the process of the incoming breath, it has met with the thinking and feeling garments of the soul as it descends in an involutive course, with the object of fusing into the newborn body—each having attracted the other with the object of discovering the 'I' concept, which is the secret of the basic principle of life on earth.

What the human being experiences through the five senses is accumulated in the mind and kept in the memory through the power of the breath, and whatever is in the mind is the product of what came through the five senses. Nevertheless, in every human being one can discover undefinable influences which have been captured from the *jinn* plane or the angelic plane. This explains why one may say of a person, "He or she is a genius," and, of another, that "He or she is angelic," when carefully studying the tendencies, dispositions, ideals and, what is more, the atmosphere of the person, all of which he or she has accumulated as a heritage from the conditions experienced prior to birth.

The soul comes on earth enriched or impoverished through its experiences within the stages of consciousness, where consciousness becomes more individualized from one plane to another. In other words, it carries light from the angelic heavens, the capacity of thought from the *jinn* plane and, on the earth, it inherits particularities from its parents and ancestors. In addition, in the physical body, which can also be considered as a universe in itself, there are also evident traces of the mineral kingdom, the vegetable kingdom and the animal kingdom, which is to say, it bears traces of all conditions through which the original lump of clay has passed. For instance, there are atoms in the body which are inherited from the mineral kingdom, others from the vegetable kingdom, and others from the animal kingdom. Indeed, even the mind shows traces these same kingdoms through which it has evolved. Through the mind, the soul is conscious of experiences received through the body. For instance, in a rigid-minded person, one can trace the dispositions of the mineral kingdom. In a supple-minded person, one can trace the dispositions of the vegetable kingdom, illustrated in the creative faculties which bring forth fruitful thoughts and deeds. The dispositions of the animal kingdom can be traced in uncontrolled passions and fears, as well as in the charm of attachment and the willingness to serve.

When manifested on the earth plane, it does not mean that the soul is disconnected from the higher spheres from whence it came. The soul radiates within the physical garb, while mostly being unaware of those outer concerns regarding whence it has come and whither it might be going. However, it is the privilege of the saintly souls and masters to be conscious of all planes simultaneously while still functioning on the physical plane.

It is said that the body is the 'Temple of God,' but this statement could be better interpreted by saying that the body is made to be the 'Temple of God.' No discomfort comes from the soul. The soul is happy by nature, the soul is happiness itself. Unhappiness comes when something goes wrong with the vehicle, the instrument, the tool with which one experiences life. Therefore, 'care of the body' is the first and the most, important principle and 'clarity of the thoughts' is also essential to enable the soul, which has come here on earth to discover the various planes of manifestation, to trace back the charm of original freedom without distraction, regardless of the burden of knowledge collected.

The greatest unhappiness comes from lack of mastery—lack of mastery of emotions, lack of mastery of thought, lack of mastery in action. Unhappiness also arises through lack of nourishment of the very fine centres of perception which, although located in the body, are of a finer substance than that of physical matter. These subtle centres of consciousness are fed with those subtle atoms of light (in other words, vibrations) which enter the body through the breath or *prana*. These subtle vibrations, which are also manifested in sounds, could be understood as being chemicals of a spiritual nature, the science of which the ancient philosophers called the 'Alchemy of Happiness'.

These subtle centres or *akashas* are like domes, wherein every sound finds an echo, and that echo goes on vibrating within as well as without. This explains why the repetition of a sacred word has not only a deep impact upon oneself and one's life circumstances, but it also spreads higher and wider and further than one could ever imagine. As it is said, "Verily, every impulse set in action, puts into movement every atom of the universe."

For the sake of convenience, the mind may be called a subtle substance, quite different from the physical understanding of matter, and the resonance of impressions received in the mind are more intense than they are when vibrating within *akashas* of a less subtle nature, such as the body. Just as there are sonorous substances, such as certain metals which have a clear resonance, whereas other objects of stone or wood do not respond as clearly to sound; so it is with finer substances and matter. Therefore, the mind is a much better vehicle for intelligence than the body.

This explains from a spiritual point of view, the difference between instinct, intuition and insight. Instinct could be seen as a resonance striking upon the body, whereas those same vibrations produce a more subtle resonance in the sphere of thought, where the mind has the ability to understand the secret message of intuition. Inspiration, coming as a gift from God, is a resonance striking the feeling heart.

The mind is a world within itself, a magic world, a world which can be easily altered and transformed. The phenomenon of the mind is great, and wonders could be performed if only one did possess the key of one's mind. Before even that, however, the first thing to seek for is the purpose of life.

Each soul has its own purpose, which is the ultimate goal and one treads either the right or the wrong path to attain it. Even though a flame is already kindled before one is born on earth, indicating the purpose of one's life and everything in the outer world points to that purpose, one is still expected to find out that secret for oneself. If one is responsive to one's intuition, or even in some circumstances to an instinctive impulse, one does discover a clear inspiration as to the purpose of one's life. Nature has taught every soul to seek its own purpose, just as it has created every soul for that purpose, and is continually indicating that goal to the soul. Everything that one does, either spiritual or material, is like a stepping stone leading to the inner purpose.

A human can intensify either the matter aspect or the spirit aspect of his or her being, but what is matter? Is it not crystallized spirit? And what is spirit? Is it not the original element, which could be likened to running water, while matter could be described as ice, each being a different condition of one and the same element?

These two polarities are again recognizable in the allegorical concepts of heaven and hell. The idea of heaven and hell exists in some form or other in all religions, providing religion a great hold upon the masses, with the aim of determining what is considered good and what is considered evil. The early scriptures were given at a time when mankind was only seeking for the fulfillment of basic wants, without attaching too much importance to concepts such as morality, justice or human rights. This explains why heaven was promised to the doer of good and the evil-doer was warned of the fires of hell, in the same way as a child is told, "Do this or that and you shall get a candy, but do not do this or that else you shall be punished."

In fact there is a heaven and a hell for each person, and what is more, the heaven of one person may be hell for another. There is no such thing as an enclosure called heaven where the virtuous ones are welcomed with rewards. Nor is there an enclosure called hell where the wrong-doers are in a state of captivity. Every person creates their own heaven or hell and, what is more, one might create one's own heaven one day, and one's own hell the next.

The soul is subject neither to birth nor death, nor does it increase nor decrease, nor evolve nor degenerate, nor is it subject to heaven or hell. One can understand this when imagining oneself standing in front of a mirror, clad in rags. It is taken for granted that the mirror holds the reflection of the rags, yet is not influenced by the concept of misery. Similarly, if one stands in front of a mirror clothed in pearls and diamonds, the image of this does fall upon the mirror, yet the mirror does not become proud. So it is with the soul, which can be neither a saint nor a sinner, as it can be neither proud nor miserable. Therefore all life's joys and sorrows and ups and downs do not affect the soul, although the soul may receive the reflections of these coming from the mirror of the mind. The power of the soul is such that it can turn any condition into a heavenly one. Not only earth, but even hell can be turned into heaven, when the soul attains the purpose of its being.

On its return, the soul passes through the same planes and states through which it pursued its route on its way to manifestation, taking along with it all the impressions which were acquired during life on earth and which constitute the garb of its individuality, until it finally frees itself from all that causes the consciousness of duality. In this state the soul becomes like a ray of sunlight, it depersonifies itself within the unconditional absolute or, in other words, the divine spirit. All the soul has borrowed through manifestation is returned to its origin. Therefore, it is natural that the physical body should return to the earth, the mind to the world of *jinns*, and the fine vibrations of the feeling heart to the angelic sphere. This is a most natural process.

Life, which is omnipresent and all-pervading, divides itself in innumerable rays as it proceeds towards manifestation, in the same way that light divides itself when it projects its rays upon darkness. Although this process has no apparent purpose, yet in this mystery lies the purpose of all purposes. The outcome of the whole manifestation is to be found in the secret of knowledge, therefore knowledge could be called the purpose of creation. It is knowledge that mystics call self-realization or God-consciousness, or even cosmic consciousness. It is for this knowledge that the whole world was created, and it is in this knowledge that the soul's purpose on earth is fulfilled.

In this connection, Hazrat Inayat Khan says, "The whole of manifestation is just like a tree sprung forth out of a divine root. Nature is like the stem, and all the aspects of nature are like the branches, the leaves, the fruit, the flowers. And from this tree again, the same seed is produced—the human soul, which was the first cause of the tree. This seed is the spirit of humanity, and as God comprehends the whole universe within the 'Divine Self,' being One, so the human contains the whole universe in miniature. The human being may most justly be called the seed of God."

Divine origin is seen in the aristocracy of the soul, whereas democracy is born out of the illusion of duality. Yet, from a mystical point of view, both ends are destined to meet in one and the same ideal—manifestation of the divine heritage in human nobility of spirit.

A flower proves to be genuine by its fragrance; a jewel proves to be genuine by its radiance; a fruit proves to be genuine by its sweetness; a soul proves to be genuine by the art of harmonizing an aristocratic origin and a democratic spirit.

What use is there of religion, of philosophy, of worship, of meditation and mysticism, if these interpretations of spirituality do not awaken the innermost inclination of the soul to reveal its divine origin which, when materialized, is expressed in a manner that is noble, a manner misunderstood by average mentalities, a manner which cannot be learned or taught, a manner which springs forth as a divine blossom?

Is the human being not the seed of God? And if so, is it not our life's purpose to bring forth divine blossoms? It is by this virtue that the soul rises from human slavery to spiritual freedom, discovering thereby the reality of its divine origin.

Here, Now and Hereafter

"Do not trouble about what you were and what you will be; realize first what you are and what you must be."
— Sangathas I,

When studying the various religions and comparing their theories and morals and beliefs regarding the reality of an afterlife, we discover that although they have different teachings on this subject, and these are expressed in still more variety, each differing from the other in appearance, yet one does perceive behind all these attempts to create a physiognomy of the afterlife, one and the same insight.

In order to emphasize this basic unity of insight (which is not the same as unity of terminology), it is most interesting to consider the following comparative illustrations. Krishna, Shiva and Buddha are said by their respective followers to have revealed what is known as the doctrine of reincarnation, whereas in the messages of the beni-Israel prophets, from Abraham to Mohammed, no dogma on this same subject has been formulated. Consequently, it is obvious that the verity of this subject is neither proven by what is clearly defined in words, nor by that which has not been made explicit in holy scriptures. Therefore, the followers of the various beliefs are not only influenced in their thoughts by what they think they understand behind the words in the respective scriptures, but what is more, the followers are endlessly the followers of the followers of the followers of this or that concept, which was originally understood in different ways according to various stages of insight.

For instance, among the Brahmins alone, there are four different interpretations of the concept of reincarnation—the interpretation made by the *Brahmachari*, by the *Grihasta*, by the *Vanaprasti* and by the *Sanyasi*, all having their own vision of the karma principle, each appropriate to their respective expectations of the future and depending on, as they put it, the principles of action and reaction or cause and effect, as they identify them in their sacred writings. The Buddhists, on the other hand, prefer to concentrate upon constant evolution in the direction of higher and higher spheres, after which there is no return. We all know the great law of beni-Israel, which is based on morals, justice, punishment and reward, permitting one to judge for oneself whether the direct consequences of an act are registered in the hereafter or not. In this regard, Jesus Christ says so beautifully, 'I will come again and receive you unto myself.' Obviously, this does not refer to the person of Christ, but to his innermost being, which through these words may be understood to be, in reality, the being of God.

Mohammed says in the Koran, "It is He who multiplied you on earth and to Him shall you be gathered." Here the principle of resurrection could be interpreted as meaning, "to make alive the souls without a physical body," in an existence which will be as clear and distinct as is our life on earth. Later, other great souls have expressed similar metaphors. Take for instance the words of Jelaluddin Rumi, who says, "Seventy-two forms I have worn and have come to witness this same Spring of continual change." This clearly refers to the divine consciousness, which appears in various images, while at the same time witnessing the changes in the environment.

As civilization advances from an intellectual point of view, the veiled illustrations of the journey which each believer interprets according to his or her own artistic insight, are more and more in need of clarification, which in no way is meant to oppose the fanatical mental construction made by those who have chosen either one or the other picture. It is certainly amusing, when confronted with people who might say that, "It is too soon to renounce the pleasures of life and perhaps this can be done in the next life," who, in so doing, put off until tomorrow what could be done today. On the other hand, the belief in reincarnation does offer great consolation to those who have lost their loved ones and who hope to see them again. And those who have not obtained successful results in their enterprises on earth, certainly do hope to experience a better result in a subsequent reincarnation. Of course, many others find good reasons, either selfish or unselfish ones, not only to believe in reincarnation, but to interpret the concept of reincarnation in such a way that it fits best their expectations and what they wish to make out of it. In other words, every believer in reincarnation weighs that subject in such a way as to turn it to his or her advantage. Furthermore, this belief has been of use to both those who believe in God and those who disbelieve. But in our age, where science, philosophy and even spirituality are searching intensely for logical interpretations of abstract concepts in the light of free thought, while at the same time venturing to recognize the divine truth hidden in back of even opposite sounding wordings, it has become so imperative to put into humble words in all sincerity, the following: There are as many truths as people believing in truth, providing they really do so.

From a purely impartial point of view, looking at the wheel of evolution, we see that human nature and inner evolution does not always rise, it also falls. Notwithstanding all the various religions which have left their mark on history, and all of which came as an appeal for love, harmony and beauty, one could perhaps say that the understanding of humanity has hardly evolved at all. Periods of evolution have been undone by periods of decay, and when looking at this picture, one can only ask oneself, "Where is the difference between the present, the hereafter and reincarnation?"

If one believes in definite distinctions between good and bad, right and wrong, sin and virtue, distinctions which in fact are only real within one's own individual concepts of such, how could one then accept another law which might offer a different interpretation concerning the route of incarnation? What seems good to one person does not necessarily seem good to another, and what seems evil to one appears to be quite natural to another. If this is so, a person who is convinced of leading a virtuous life could certainly not expect to be confronted with punishment when reincarnated if it did happen that a reverse judgement prevailed in the hereafter. And if so, where is the value of self-contentment?

Since we are even ignorant of what occurs on other planets, how can we claim to know what occurs in the heavens in the hereafter? Would it not be better to use one's time, concentration and energy in making the best of one's life here on earth, where everything that exists is, in fact, in perpetual change, transformation, and eternal recycling from the beginning to the end. These recycling processes take place within our sphere of comprehension, that is to say, within all those stages of understanding perceived through our five senses, and are thereby logically definable.

Nevertheless, since matter and spirit are not opposite concepts, but are only two end-points of one same line, points which in fact meet each other in the infinite, and a line which is made out of infinite degrees of evolution of matter toward spirit, and involution of spirit toward matter. Therefore, there is every reason to believe that there is a reality at an abstract level which our understanding ventures to place at a material level. Although we are not able to define it in words, in ciphers or in energy values, yet we are granted the favour of perceiving reality according to the level of our inner realization. Therefore, let us leave the reality of God to God, and leave the reality of humanity to human beings and, in so doing, avoid any speculative theories which only lead to confusion, contradiction, disillusionment and even more ignorance. As it is said, "Make God a reality, and God will make you the truth."

Whatever diversity may appear to be among religions and beliefs, the motive of all is one and the same—to cultivate the human heart with the purpose of discovering divine love within. From time to time, the 'Spirit of Guidance' drew the attention of mankind to the beauty of God in God's creation, in the trees, the rocks, the lakes, the mountains, the streams, sometimes even in the animals, the birds, or even the sacred mythological beings, at periods when mankind was not intellectually in a position to conceive God in any other shape or image than one corresponding to one of God's creatures. These conceptions developed in time to the recognition of higher personifications, such as holy ones and God-conscious ones.

Obviously, in this recognition, the object of love of each person corresponds to one's own standard of beauty, thereby giving birth to the various personifications of God, known and developed by all religions all down the ages. If there is a purpose in life, it is certainly not to formulate the hereafter within the limitations of one's own mind world, but it is to open one's eyes to the vision of that which is already there—the 'Divine Presence.' The more we surrender ourselves to the 'Divine Presence' and the more our consciousness is capable of losing itself in the 'Divine Presence,' the more the hereafter will be revealed to us in the present. In other words, the hereafter is, at the same time, the past, the present and the future, which means that when forgetting oneself in the thought of the 'Divine Presence,' one is in fact living at the same time in the past, the present and the future simultaneously.

Light and Life
An interpretation of the Sangithas

The Hindu term for a mystic is *Antarajnani*, the knower of the worlds unseen, and the Hindu word *akasha* means the heavens within, as a capacity or receptacle of all different aspects of life according to one's consciousness. The all-pervading light is self-subsistent—it is contained within itself and it manifests when it can find a capacity where it can be expressed as an individual point of radiance. The subsequent reaction to this individualization is a further illumination, as it is said in the Koran, "I have created thee with my light, and from thy light all is created." In this, is the secret of the Hindu concept of trinity (*Trimurti*). First, there is the all-pervading light; second, the light when concentrated in one point; and third, the light shining within itself and thereby illuminating all things, reflecting in all things, strengthening and invigorating all things, in the same way that it is the nature of the sun to help the plants to grow and flourish.

Light is silent and, in its original nature, inactive. This condition of inertia is called in Hindu terms *sattva*. The beginning of the activity of light is the assumption of individuality, and it is this individual capacity which allows the activity of the all-pervading life to become intelligible. In the Bible it is said, "First was the word and the word was God," which could be understood to mean that the all-pervading light, which is silent, has manifested itself first in the realm of sound. In the Vedanta, this is referred to as *Nada Brahma* or 'divine vibration'. In the Koran it is said, "Allah is the Light of heaven and earth."

That which we recognize as space or what we call vacuum is all light. It manifests when vibrations unite and when atoms group together. It is audible when it acts as vibrations, and it is visible when it manifests as atoms. The question as to how the secret of the universe could be found within oneself, which is like a drop in the ocean, may be answered thus, that the drop is the ocean in miniature, and the one who studies the drop, studies the ocean. The saying of Christ, "Straight is the gate and narrow is the way," speaks of the centres within, which seem a narrow gate compared with the outer world which is so vast. However, when one discovers the self within, one is thereby discovering the whole universe.

The Mystery of Breath
A Practice Called "Shagal"
An interpretation of the Sangithas

Life is light, and light is omnipotent and omnipresent. It is the comparison of light that is concentrated and of light that is spread out, which accounts for the whole scenery of creation. For instance, when centred, light manifests as luminosity and, when scattered, it manifests as movement. The soul, heart, mind and body are different grades of radiance focused in limited forms, thoughts and feelings. The human being is so constituted that, by the help of the organs of the senses and the stimulus of light and sound, one feels and knows all that is around one, and one connects with all around by opening the channels of communication between oneself and others. For instance, the voice opens a communication which penetrates through the hearing of another and so reaches the heart of a listener. Therefore, this life can be lived still more fully by awakening faculties which have hitherto remained covered and unnurtured by the breath, just as there may be a piece of ground which has lain waste and barren for want of water or, where there is water, but which the light of the sun does not reach.

The breath has the tendency to reach outwards, but the further it spreads the more it loses its magnetism, just as light diminishes in luminosity at a distance and then, by comparison, may be termed darkness. In reality, there is no such thing as darkness, but only lesser degrees of light, which again become brighter and brighter as one turns back in the direction of the source of radiance. The breath is also comparable to light in this sense, that it can have an influence on all those who are sensitive to its magnetism. Indeed, the intensity of that magnetism varies according to the radiance of the breath, which finds its source within the inner roots of the true self. In other words, the radiance in the breath is all-pervading, both in the inner world and the outer world. What is more, this radiance can be directed to a distant receiver or focused on a given spot, illuminating all within its path with magnetic rays strengthened by the energy of thought.

The breath is the vehicle upon which the consciousness rides out into the world during the exhalation, and upon the inhalation, the consciousness returns, loaded with impressions which are registered in the mechanisms of the five senses, before reaching the coordinating centres of the mind where these finally become intelligible.

In this process, the breath is like a bridge connecting the outer world and the inner world, which is the spectator of all senses.

Breath is the most important power regulating the course of our lives, or in other words breath is, really speaking, life itself. Therefore, those who ignore the mysteries of breath are regrettably deprived of the basic knowledge of life, from a scientific viewpoint as well as with regard to spiritual insight. Either one has control over the breath, in which case one acquires a humble hold over the unknown, or one is unfortunately led by the uncontrolled power of one's own life-giving breath.

Breath can be disciplined to various rhythmic patterns and also focused so as to trace specific, mentally visualized geometric shapes. Once this has been practised, the next step is the appropriate adaptation of the power of breath to all circumstances. This, of course, implies making a wise use of the different characteristics of breath as known in Swara Yoga. For instance, according to the theory of yoga *kundaly-upanishad*, when the positive *pingala* or *jelal* vibrations of the breath current manifest more pronouncedly during exhalation through the right nostril, this indicates a creative and expressive condition, physically, mentally and emotionally. When the negative *ida* or *jemal* vibrations manifest more pronouncedly during exhalation through the left nostril, this favours a perceptive and receptive condition. However, when both positive and negative vibrations in the breath (*purusha-prakriti*) flow together (*shushumna* or *kemal*) through both nostrils during the exhalation, either a chaotic situation resulting from a clash of opposite energies may be expected or, conversely, the two opposite energies might harmonize, creating thereby, a balanced and most elevating meditative condition which only persists, however, during peaceful attunement.

Another aspect of the power of breath is in its special function of absorbing subtle vibrations of the five elements in the cosmos and channelling these, day and night, upon its ebb and flow within the pathways or *nadis* of the breath. In this process, the influence of the earth element is steadiness; the water element is progress onwards; the fire element is excitement or destruction; the air element is receptivity, inspiration; the ether element is spiritual attunement. Among many other esoteric methods, the breath can be purified through the influence of the element upon the inhalation and exhalation. Sitting cross-legged or, better, standing, one absorbs, from space, the subtle vibrations of the different elements in turn, holding these in thought, within appropriate *chakras*. On the exhalation, the impurities therein are cleansed through the mystical touch of the magnetism of the chosen element.

Breathing practices are best sustained with the help of rhythmic patterns which discipline the alternating flow of inhaling and exhaling energy, thus providing the breath with an *akasha* of measure, time and shape. Hidden in this discipline is the understanding of the individualization of breath, that is to say, the capture of the *prana*-energy of the cosmos in an appropriate receiver for the sake of life itself. This secret is the key to the process of resignation to the divine will or, in other words, it is in itself the mystical purpose of all practices done by the seeker of truth on the spiritual path. The object of the seeker is not necessarily the attainment of power or the achievement of inspiration, it is to touch the depth of life, that plane of existence whence springs every activity manifesting through different channels.

By the practice of *Shagal* one withdraws the breath from one direction and sends it in another direction, meaning that instead of projecting the breath outward, one is directing it inwardly. Breath is life, light and sound, in itself. Therefore, in the Vedanta, breath is called *Suram* or *Swara*, meaning sound. *Shagal* awakens the awareness of the vibrations within, in that inner being which may be understood as the root of all senses. Among the many benefits that one derives from *Shagal*, the simplest is that one gains control over all the senses which are otherwise slaves to every external call. By a constant practise of *Shagal*, one is able to draw a cover over those senses which one does not specially wish to experience at the moment. The one who is master over body, mind and heart becomes a valid instrument to experience life fully. In every centre or *chakra* the breath resounds to a specific tone and when these tones are distinct, not only does the body become radiant and the senses become acute, but also one's innermost being becomes responsive to a new level of consciousness.

The more we receive impressions from all planes of consciousness, the more we receive knowledge from within, where all knowledge collects, which is the true secret of inspiration. *Shagal* offers the recognition of an energy with two opposite directions experienced in one and the same consciousness—that which draws inward, and that which draws outward from within. For instance, when blocking the senses one is, so to speak, pulling down a veil over the outer impressions, in an effort to open a contact with the energy within. In this practice, the working of the senses is reversed. That is to say, one is drawing from within instead of from outside, with this difference—that from which we draw from within is the very source of all sensorial energy, whereas that which is received from outside, although sustained by the energy of the cosmos, wears an inescapable veil of mental substance, because our mind inevitably distorts our perceptions in giving them an identity.

When closing the hearing, one listens to the unstruck sound of the cosmos, then audible within as '*Hu*'. When closing the sight, one searches for the inner light, revealed as luminosity with no relationship to any material brilliancy. When closing off the taste, one replaces it by an incoming feeling of savouring the nature of values unknown to the tongue, which are spiritually related to the ecstasy felt in the power of silence. When closing the nostrils and thereby blocking the incoming flow of breath, one is merging the self-consciousness into the very same substance, *prana,* which has been thereby held within and which is then revealed, in the absence of the self (now dissolved in the divine fragrance of the abstract spheres), as the only true reality. The nature of the *Shagal* practice is such that, during all stages, one is in subtle contact with the presence of a central consciousness and, in that experience, the fifth sense, the touch, is sublimated to a higher level of perception, different from the ordinary understanding of the concept of touch.

When the five senses—hearing, sight, taste, touch and the olfactory perception——have each been inwardly experienced, one can then proceed with two advanced aspects of *Shagal*. The first is to block all senses simultaneously, as a practice. The second, to be continually attuned during one's daily activities, to all variations in nature's scenery, in an attitude of self-denial. However, it is essential to indicate that these meditative practices cannot have any effect unless they are done in sincere humility without any self-assertion or material purpose.

The physician who discovers the heart of the patient can know more and better about the general condition than the one who looks for the pain in the affected part. In the same way, by the practice of *Shagal*, one gets to the heart of things, where one can see the seedling of success and failures, where one can see the signs of forthcoming joy or pain. In practising *Shagal,* one learns to see independently of the eyes and to hear independently of the ears. As soon as the senses achieve this independence from their physical instrument of experience, they begin to see and hear beyond the limitations of these, and the area of consciousness becomes widened. The sight, which previously saw only to a limited horizon, now sees much further than before. Similarly the hearing, that could hear by the help of the ears, so much and no more, now hears, after mastering *Shagal*, much more than ever before.

The soul is always tempted to look outward for its experience and therefore it remains unaware of the inner being. It turns its back, so to speak, on the inner life, absorbed in the vision of the external through the five senses. In *Shagal*, one closes the window through which the soul is accustomed to look out on the external world. The soul then sees before it a different sphere altogether, yet a sphere that has been within it all the while. Here the soul has a wonderful vision, visible and audible, and the light and power of this vision stays with the soul, illuminating the different planes of consciousness. It is like coming in the daylight to a room which the soul had once visited in the darkness of night. Everything in life becomes clear, and that which once confused the soul is now solved.

The *Religion* of the Sufi is the cry of the heart,

The *Ideal* of the Sufi is spiritual consciousness,

The *Goal* of the Sufi is self-realization,

The *God* of the Sufi is the divine presence within,

The *Path* of the Sufi is brotherhood and sisterhood,

The *Manner* of the Sufi is inner nobility,

The *Art* of the Sufi is personality,

The *Charm* of the Sufi is humility,

The *Moral* of the Sufi is beneficence,

The *Attitude* of the Sufi is forgiving,

The *Beloved* of the Sufi is love itself.

Achevé d'imprimer
chez
Marc Veilleux,
Imprimeur à Boucherville,
en octobre mil neuf cent quatre-vingt-seize